Journeys of Entrepreneurs

Stories of Risk Takers Who Improved Themselves, Their
Employees, Their Customers, and Their Communities

by Lee Rice

OPEN BOOK
EDITIONS
A Berrett–Koehler Partner

Journeys of Entrepreneurs
Stories of Risk Takers Who Improved Themselves, Their
Employees, Their Customers, and Their Communities

iUniverse books may be ordered through booksellers or by contacting:

iUniverse
1663 Liberty Drive
Bloomington, IN 47403
www.iuniverse.com
1-800-Authors (1-800-288-4677)

Because of the dynamic nature of the Internet, any web addresses or links contained in this book may have changed since publication and may no longer be valid. The views expressed in this work are solely those of the author and do not necessarily reflect the views of the publisher, and the publisher hereby disclaims any responsibility for them.

Any people depicted in stock imagery provided by Thinkstock are models, and such images are being used for illustrative purposes only.

Certain stock imagery © Thinkstock.

ISBN: 978-1-4620-2874-0 (sc)
ISBN: 978-1-4620-2876-4 (hc)
ISBN: 978-1-4620-2875-7 (e)

Library of Congress Control Number: 2011917039

Printed in the United States of America

iUniverse rev. date: 10/31/2011

To my grandchildren—Julia, Andrew, Emma, and Matthew
May they have the opportunity to become entrepreneurs.

Contents

Introduction

During the Great Recession of 2008–2010, when the real threat of economic and financial collapse confronted the US economy, some observers believed that America's great capitalist system was near the end of its long journey. However, with heavy doses of government funds, the injection of hundreds of billions of dollars from the Federal Reserve into the economy, and the confidence of many businesspeople, the United States was rescued from the precipice of economic failure.

No doubt, federal bailout plans from both the Bush and Obama administrations were critical to saving the economy, which was nearly destroyed by the housing bust that excessive bank lending and politicians who supported risky mortgage loans fueled. However, a sustained economy recovery, one that generates jobs on a long-term basis, requires the ideas and innovations of American entrepreneurs who have created economic growth in our nation since its inception.

I define an entrepreneur as a person who launches a new business venture and accepts responsibility for its outcome. But this book also profiles a few leaders who did not start their businesses; rather, they took charge of existing ventures, some of which were near failure or required a new management team, and made them successful by elevating their enterprises to higher levels.

The "Invisible Hand"

Investing in a new business is critical to the creation of jobs. In both *The Theory of Moral Sentiments* and *The Wealth of Nations,* the eighteenth-century economist Adam Smith discussed his famous idea of the *invisible hand,* which defines the entrepreneurs in this book:

> By preferring the support of domestic to that of foreign industry, he intends only his own security, and by directing that industry in such a manner as its produce may be of the greatest value, he intends only his own gain, and he is in this, as in many other cases, led by an invisible hand to promote an end which was no part of his intention ... By pursuing his own interest he frequently promotes that of the society more effectually than when he really intends to promote it.[1]

Smith's famous idea of the invisible hand refers to the unintended consequences that result from actions by the investor or entrepreneur. Thus, if I invest my capital in a new business venture to generate wealth, the following can occur:

- The financial condition of my life and my family's lives will improve.

- Jobs will be created for my employees that will boost economic growth.

- Taxes will be paid to all levels of government to pay for services rendered to its citizens.

- Consumers will benefit from the products and/or services that my enterprise creates.

Also, and very importantly, the successful entrepreneur will be able to engage in outreach within the community and help others who may be less fortunate.

As I attempt to demonstrate in this book, the actions of the sixteen entrepreneurs in the following chapters are manifestations of Smith's famous and oft-cited example of the invisible hand. This book profiles entrepreneurs in both small and larger businesses, most of whom I have known for many years, and discusses the characteristics that define these risk takers. I chose the entrepreneurs who are profiled in this book because, not only do they embody Smith's famous invisible hand, they have been successful in their careers. Additionally, they:

- Demonstrated the importance of successful innovation when it was required

- Provided excellent customer service

- Overcame setbacks and disappointments

- Focused on improving employee relations

- Made contributions to the communities in which they live and operate

"Creative Destruction"

In *Return to Prosperity: How America Can Regain Its Superpower Status,* Arthur Laffer and Stephen Moore gave meaning to Smith's invisible hand. "Entrepreneurs not only carry other people with them as investors in their journeys to super wealth, they also provide meaningful jobs and high-quality products at low cost."[2] Furthermore, they wrote:

Consumers and workers benefit above and beyond where they otherwise would have been. These entrepreneurs bring new "disruptive" technologies to the market that reorganizes the entire concept of product and production.[3]

The Austrian economist, Joseph Schumpeter, referred to this disruptive process as *creative destruction*, which he called "the essential fact about capitalism."[4]

Readers of this book will learn that some of the entrepreneurs in the following chapters have embraced change that fits the definition of being disruptive and has simultaneously improved their companies, enabled them to deliver a better product to their customers, and enhanced the financial condition of their own lives and their employees as well. Lending support to Art Laffer and Steve Moore's book, management consultant and author, Tom Peters, in his excellent book, *The Circle of Innovation*, wrote, "Destruction is cool. Change the organization and recruit diversity."[5] In a modern competitive economy such as ours, it is critically important to be innovative, flexible and embrace customer service with passion. If entrepreneurs do not embrace these factors, they may run the risk of not being in business to provide services to their customers.

My undergraduate college economics professor, R. Pierce Lumpkin, was a believer in Smith's invisible hand idea as the central driving force behind business investment. He would always remind his classes that the primary factors of production in a society consisted of land, labor, capital, and the entrepreneur. Consequently, all of these factors create wealth and have the possibility to improve the lives of other members of society as well.

The Small Business Administration (SBA), which provides business loans and financial advice to many small businesses of different sizes and types, defines a small business as having fewer than five hundred employees, which applies to all businesses profiled in this book with the exception of two. Nevertheless, the success of Dario Marquez, whose much larger company, MVM, is described in chapter 1, may have positive lessons for readers who aspire to be successful leaders of larger companies. His company has also benefited the citizens of Virginia and the United States, as readers will learn.

But Dario Marquez is not the only entrepreneur in this book who has operated a larger company with more than five hundred employees. Bobby Ukrop, for example, the former president of a popular and very successful grocery store chain with twenty-five units, oversaw six thousand employees before he and his brother James sold the company in 2010. Ukrop now owns and operates a newly created food manufacturing business called Ukrop's Homestyle Foods that employs approximately five hundred people.

Americans have long had a love affair with small businesses. According to Mansel Blackford, in his *History of Small Business in America*, smaller businesses have been important not only in an economic sense, but in a cultural sense as well.[6] Moreover, he adds, "More than the cultures of other nations, that of the U.S. has developed a business culture."[7]

In a March 18, 2011 *Richmond Times-Dispatch* news story, Karen Mills, head of the SBA, said that half the people in the country (the United States) work for a small business and 60 percent of new jobs are in small business.[8]

The independence, the freedom in which to operate, and the chance for personal success, all of these are responsible for luring many would-be entrepreneurs into starting their own businesses and demonstrating the validity of Adam Smith's invisible hand. But despite the challenges that larger businesses in our history presented, combined with the fact that more small businesses fail than survive, one has to be impressed with the remarkable resiliency of many entrepreneurs.

From the beginning of our country in the seventeenth century, small businesses were predominant. However, the creation of railroads, the birth of steam engines, the development of the telegraph, and rapid growth in the population of America, including the rise of larger capital-intensive companies, all of these developments posed a threat to smaller- and medium-sized enterprises in the late nineteenth century. The fortunes of small businesses generally declined during the Depression of the 1930s and both WWI and WWII. Even the recession of 2008 to 2010 caused the demise of many smaller businesses.

But importantly, in his book, Mansel Blackford wrote that small businesses remained part of the American scene as the twenty-first century opened.[9] Even in the last quarter of the twentieth century, Blackford wrote that small firms generated a significant share of America's new jobs and they "remained important as sources of innovation, particularly in the commercialization of new processes and products."[10]

Female Entrepreneurs

One important development in the history of small businesses in the latter part of the twentieth century, according to Blackford, was the increase in opportunities for women. "From the late 1970s through the 1990s, women formed new businesses, nearly all of which were small, at a much higher rate than men."[11] My book describes the success of women entrepreneurs such as:

- The inspirational Sharon Dabney-Wooldridge, founder and president of the very successful janitorial company, KleaneKareTeam

- Suzanne Woltsensholme, president of the popular catering company, Homemades by Suzanne

- Teresa Mason, the energetic founder and owner of Breath of Fresh Air, which offers lessons in health care to the public

- Marie Kelleher, chairperson of family-owned Kelleher Corporation, a heating, air-conditioning, and plumbing company, which her late husband, Michael, started

Other chapters consist of successful entrepreneurs such as:

- Patrick Duffeler, winery owner

- David Watson, machinist and engineer

- Michael O'Neil, health care entrepreneur

- Al Katz, retirement community and nursing home president

- Stewart Hargrove, business insurance advocate

- Mark Motley, auctioneer

- Wayne Hazzard, electrical and general contractor

- Michael Kasmir and Dan Wolford, staffing company founders

- The late David Ward, contractor and voting machine entrepreneur

While Michael Kelleher and David Ward are deceased, their compelling stories live on and contain lessons for younger entrepreneurs and others who seek to create their own businesses.

Also significant to the success of the entrepreneur is the importance of not being afraid to fail or make mistakes because nearly everyone is going to. As the reader will learn from this book, even the most successful entrepreneur made mistakes. However, all learned from their errors and emerged stronger and wiser in the aftermath of their miscues.

The aforementioned author and management consultant Tom Peters wrote that Walmart founder, Sam Walton, was not afraid of making errors. Quoting Wal-Mart CEO David Glass, who knew Walton for thirty years, he said:

The one thing about Sam that really stands out is that he's not afraid to make mistakes, mess something up. He gets on with something new tomorrow morning. He doesn't waste time looking back.[12]

In his important book, *Innovate the Future: A Radical New Approach to IT Innovation,* former Hewlett-Packard chief technologist, David Croslin, wrote about the critical importance of taking care of the customer. In a January 2011 interview with *Entrepreneur,* Croslin said the iPhone, for example, is really about the customer. He said that going back to the basics can fix a lot of things. Croslin said that mobile phone companies kept trying to top each other with features that most people never used.[13] But the iPhone was designed to meet these problems.

Saving Time and Money and Simplifying Life

Croslin believed the customer must see the transformative value in a product or service. Importantly, buyers will not buy a product unless it saves time and money and simplifies their lives.[14] Unfortunately, Croslin said that many companies end up trying to please themselves or beat competitors rather than considering their customers.[15]

The future of the economy of Virginia, neighboring states, and the United States, in my opinion, largely depends on empowering entrepreneurs and removing impediments to their efforts. In a special program on "Restoring the American Dream" on CNN on March 6, 2011, journalist and commentator, Fareed Zakaria said:

> The U.S. needs new entrepreneurs to generate more jobs and growth, not only to ensure more expansion in our own economy, but to compete against other nations, particularly China, India, and other Asian nations who threaten to surpass us.[16]

Most observers agree that job creation is more likely to occur among small start-up ventures as opposed to large corporations, many of whom downsize and even trim employment if sales do not increase. In her hugely popular book, *Atlas Shrugged*, Ayn Rand quoted her hero, John Galt, who, after returning to lead the capitalists after the socialist enemy is banished, sounded the call to all would-be entrepreneurs when he declared, "With the sign of the dollar as our symbol—the sign of free trade and free minds—we will move to reclaim this country."[17]

Galt is right when he refers to a renaissance of free minds. The birth of an idea normally spurs innovations and the creation of an enterprise.

To be sure, entrepreneurship is not an easy task. Rather, as this book seeks to demonstrate, it involves lots of hard work. None of the entrepreneurs in this book have failed and been forced to close down their businesses, but some have suffered setbacks. Sadly, however, many would-be entrepreneurs enter the task with no well-thought-out plan. They believe that becoming an entrepreneur only involves hard work.

But entrepreneurs should be aware of my dad's venture into entrepreneurship. He owned and operated a small drugstore and lunch business in a small town in the historic Northern Neck of Virginia. He worked very hard and drew praise from the customers who patronized his store. However, a catastrophic fire in 1952 that began across the street from his enterprise and burned down one-third of all stores in the business district of Kilmarnock, Virginia, destroyed his store. Sadly, he had failed to purchase an adequate amount of fire insurance that would have enabled him to rebuild his store, and he was forced to work for a larger company in a completely different area of concentration. Thus, his own dream of entrepreneurship was dealt a fatal blow.

In her excellent best-selling book, *Entrepreneur Equation*, investment banker and author, Carol Roth, wrote:

Potential entrepreneurs are continually lured into businesses with a false picture (or at least a gross misunderstanding) of what entrepreneurship is, with unrealistic promises regarding the potential financial and other rewards they can gain from operating businesses, and with no means to assess whether the investment justifies the risk, or if the opportunity is appropriate for them.[18]

All potential entrepreneurs should read Roth's book because it offers a reality check. She said that unsuccessful entrepreneurs usually start their businesses without first going through a screening process because the game of entrepreneurship has changed and being an entrepreneur today, particularly a successful one, is more difficult than it has ever been.[19]

During the three decades I worked in the financial industry— first in banking, next as a stockbroker, and finally as a commercial insurance agent and auditor of workers' compensation business insurance policies—I met hundreds of entrepreneurs, many of whom were successful and others who made mistakes that led to their failure. Based on my own business experience and observations of entrepreneurs, combined with my educational background in history and economics, I believe my book will be helpful to readers who desire to gain knowledge of risk takers as well as younger persons seeking a career that might lead to success for them.

Dario Marquez, Security Expert

I'm comfortable with risk.

Anyone knowing Dario Marquez during his youth could be forgiven if they did not think he would become successful in life. Abandoned by his father early in life and living in Dover, New Jersey, where there were only a few Puerto Ricans, Marquez's mother raised him during the final years of WWII. He said his mother worked in a factory to support her family. Indeed, he said that the values he carried and the spirit came from his mom.

Despite the less than satisfactory economic circumstances in his early years, Marquez believed his mother carried the entrepreneurial spirit and the gene because her father was a business owner. Moreover, Marquez had a dream at a young age to become an entrepreneur. He said:

> I would sit in my mother's car and daydream of what I thought I would become ... I had an image of a man with his back to me, carrying a clipboard and wearing a perfectly laundered shirt with French cuffs as he walked down the middle of what was a manufacturing plant.

The attire and demeanor of the man in Marquez's daydream indicated he was in charge. Marquez believed his dreams would help liberate him from his social and economic environment.

As the years advanced, Marquez read much about American

industrialists who became his heroes and role models: Henry Ford, J.C. Penney, Andrew Carnegie, and, very importantly, Napoleon Hill. Hill worked his way through Georgetown Law School and wrote *Think and Grow Rich*. He was an early pioneer in the studies of personal success literature.

One particular story Marquez had not forgotten was Hill's interview with Andrew Carnegie, which lasted for three days as opposed to an anticipated time of one hour. Moreover, what impressed Marquez was Hill's belief that everything starts with an idea. Marquez said these images or ideas provided hope for his own future. Furthermore, he said he developed the "Lee Iacocca fire in the belly" idea to become an entrepreneur and be successful.

MVM CEO, Dario Marquez

Becoming a Secret Service Agent

Following college and graduate school, Marquez searched for an idea that would provide the impetus to become a successful leader, comparable to the man in his dreams. First, however, he had to find a job. A friend suggested he apply for a position at the US Secret Service, which was in the process of seeking new recruits. Thus, from 1972 to 1979, Marquez began his professional career as a special agent where he served under the administrations of Presidents Nixon, Ford, and Carter. He was also assigned to provide protection for not only heads of state, but Secretary of State Henry Kissinger and former New York Governor and Vice President Nelson Rockefeller as well.

But to prepare for a career in security and fulfill his boyhood dream of becoming an entrepreneur, Marquez received a bachelor of science degree in business administration at Southeastern University, finished graduate studies in criminal justice at Long Island University in New York, and completed the US Secret Service Law Enforcement Training Institute in 1972.

During his nearly eight years at the Secret Service, Marquez mastered and implemented the fundamental principles of personal and physical security and logistics management. As an agent, he attended presidential conventions, one of which in Miami was marked by riots. Marquez also worked with many other agents, a few of whom were later assigned to protect former President Ronald Reagan on the fateful day of March 30, 1981, when John Hinckley Jr. shot the president following his departure from the Washington Hilton where he delivered a speech to AFL-CIO representatives.

While Marquez did not protect President Reagan, nevertheless, the story about the agents who did save his life may be of interest since he attended the same classes and knew them very well. Agent Tim McCarthy, who trained with Marquez and attended classes that led to his job as a Secret Service agent, received a bullet in his abdomen as he fell across Reagan's body to absorb any further shots that might be intended for the president from Hinckley's revolver. Following the attempted assassination, another Secret Service agent or detail leader, Jerry Parr, who had been assigned to protect the president, discovered a bullet had punctured Reagan's lung, prompting Parr to divert the presidential motorcade to nearby George Washington Hospital rather than return to the White House. Marquez said Parr's quick decision saved Reagan's life. Furthermore, Marquez said Parr had the power to lead the president of the United States. Importantly, he concluded the agent took control of events and made decisions that saved the life of the most important leader in the world. "It is amazing the amount of power an agent can really have and how really boring the job can be (on some occasions)."

During his career as a Secret Service agent, Marquez said most agents spend their days performing investigative work, which the public might not know. However, he added the most exciting, fun, and challenging times in his career were the early days when he worked in New York City as an undercover agent in the counterfeit squad. His ability to speak Spanish was an enormous benefit in this aspect of his career. "When you work with a counterfeit squad, there are also drugs that are linked to terrorist activities," Marquez added.

> In his eight years as a Secret Service agent, Marquez, according to his company's website, had: [M]astered and applied the principles of personal and physical security and logistics management, which are the hallmarks of the United States Service … which meet the needs of private and public sector clients in the areas of security personnel management, security training, executive protection, criminal and civil investigations, technical security, and security risk assessments and studies.

From Agent to Entrepreneur

Marquez saw his years as a Secret Service agent as an important step on his journey to become an entrepreneur, the type of entrepreneur he longed for since the days as a young boy when he sat in his mother's car on Crystal Street in Dover and dreamed of his future. Because he really desired to own his business, in 1979, he founded and became CEO of his own company, MVM, a large and privately owned security company that employs thirty-five hundred security professionals worldwide and is based near Dulles Airport. MVM is very fortunate to have two senior vice presidents—David Westrate and Louie McKinney—who bring many years of experience in the security industry and add real depth to its top management.

Marquez is a very articulate, disciplined, and determined man. Like his boyhood visionary, the heroic leader who walked along the factory floor, he also wears distinctively French laundered shirts and is in charge of a large growing company. His story is remarkably similar, in part, to the journey of the nineteenth-century American folk hero, Horatio Alger, who worked his way to the top of the ladder and motivated other entrepreneurs in their journeys through life.

In the beginning, MVM attempted to work for mostly large companies in the private sector, but he learned his company could not count on consistent growth from these enterprises. Therefore, to gain a wider market share and become more effective, MVM has grown into a diversified governmental contractor on a global basis. Since terrorism and threats to security can and do occur anywhere regardless of national boundaries, MVM seeks to respond to challenges at any time. Accordingly, its employees protect the citizens and institutions of the United States across the world.

Protecting American Citizens

At various periods in its history, MVM has provided services to an impressive group of governmental agencies and institutions that include:

- Departments of Homeland Security, Justice, State, Defense, US Navy, Air Force, Commerce, and Energy

- Drug Enforcement Administration (DEA)

- US Marshals Service

- Internal Revenue Service (IRS)

- Immigration and Customs Enforcement (ICE)

- Bureau of Prisons

- Federal Emergency Management Agency (FEMA)

- Federal Protection Service

- National Institutes of Health (NIH)

- Smithsonian Institute

It has also provided protection services to Ford Motor Company, *Time*, and the Rockefeller family.

Under Marquez's leadership, MVM has developed an excellent reputation for developing security programs that address special challenges. In 1987, for example, MVM obtained a US government contract to install security protocols at the United States embassy in Moscow following an internal investigation that revealed foreign intelligence agents had penetrated it. In the aftermath of its success in Moscow, MVM assisted the US government in adopting the security protocols of the Omnibus Diplomatic Security and Antiterrorism Act at American embassies across the world.

MVM provided the Haitian government in Port-au-Prince with trainers and advisors in 1994 to set up a presidential protective program to prepare for the return of President Aristide. MVM continued to provide these services during the transition of power for the administration of President Preval. Two years later, MVM was the first American company to supply security to a seated US ambassador, who, at the time, was Ambassador Robert Frowick in

Bosnia, a country that was at war between 1992 and 1995 following the death of Marshall Tito and the breakup of Yugoslavia, a multinational country he had ruled for decades with an iron fist before it split into different ethnic groups.

Like many successful entrepreneurs, Marquez does not fear innovation because he understands that companies must change to remain alive. In fact, MVM's decision to work for governmental agencies instead of mostly corporate clients was a manifestation of being innovative and recognizing the nature of the threat to national security. Moreover, this decision has enabled MVM to survive and help protect Americans most anywhere in the world. Marquez said they had to adapt in order to survive because he realized all Americans had become targets of terrorism following the Iranian hostage crisis during the final years of the Carter presidency in 1979 and 1980 and other events, including some that have occurred within the United States.

The Silver Eagle Group

To continue the process of adapting to the changing world, one that continues to pose threats to all Americans, Marquez and his four sons created another company called the Silver Eagle Group in 2008. Marquez said forming a new company is a big risk, but it was necessary to enable them to expand their service offerings and continue to grow. He added he was comfortable with risk, as he discussed the reasons for creating the Silver Eagle Group. He said he had the courage of his convictions as he elaborated further on his idea of the entrepreneur, but also on the need to meet new challenges from threats to all Americans. Marquez said that standing still is not an option, as he defended his decision to spend millions of dollars to embark on what he called "innovative training" in a new company within MVM.

Looking to the future, Marquez said his investment in the Silver

Eagle Group would be either based on reality or missing the mark as he assessed the threats to all Americans. Located in the same building with the parent company, MVM, the Silver Eagle Group Training Facility perhaps offers the most comprehensive and innovative self-defense education and specialized training program in the United States. Importantly, local, state, and federal law enforcement personnel as well as the public at large engage in training at its Northern Virginia location.

The Silver Eagle Group has built a state-of-the-art training facility featuring three indoor shooting ranges that consist of two twenty-five-yard ranges and one fifty-yard range with ten lanes each. These ranges, according to its website, allow shooters to practice with pistol, rifle, or shotgun, using calibers of up to fifty BMG. Furthermore, a multi-stage filtration system independently ventilates the ranges, ensuring shooter health and comfort.

Included in the facility, the Silver Eagle Group features a retail section that sells firearms, ammunition, and rentals and accessories. Gunsmith services are offered for weapon cleanings, repairs, and those who desire to customize their weapons. Shooting ranges are not the only features in this attractive facility. Self-defense courses are offered in a specially created mat room that contains matted floors and walls as well as boxing bags and other mixed martial arts equipment. Also contained in the facilities are four classrooms as well as a twenty-two thousand-square foot scenario training area that contains a two-story townhouse, a replica of a school and office suite, and a laser technology training area. The training facility, coupled with the scenario area, seeks to instruct the student in a realistic training environment. Marquez said his company hired martial arts experts to add combatives and mixed martial arts training alongside the weapons instructions.

The Silver Eagle Group's services have become more relevant and necessary in a country that experienced:

- Terrorist attacks on September 11, 2001, that Al-Qaeda organized and carried out

- A single gunman killing thirty-three students at Virginia Tech in Blacksburg, Virginia, in April 2007

- An American-born Muslim soldier killing thirteen people and wounding twenty-nine others at Fort Hood in November 2009

These mass killings that occurred in the United States demonstrate the need for an effective response. Marquez believes we can all fall victim to a criminal or terrorist act. He added that the training philosophy of the Silver Eagle Group is to teach the student to be aware of the surroundings, think clearly under stress, and respond appropriately. The response could be to find an avenue of escape, if possible, or to use their own marksmanship or martial arts skills, if necessary.

Marquez's own marksmanship skills support his comments on training students and officers in his company's shooting ranges. In fact, during my interview, he displayed a silver pistol trophy that members of his staff presented to him as a result of achieving a perfect score on a pistol qualification course.

Training Everyone to Meet the Threat

Elaborating on the critical importance of the Silver Eagle Group, Marquez said, "We teach the student, who may be a civilian, police officer, or military personnel, to respond appropriately under pressure" because, he said that, if you cannot execute under pressure, you are done. He acknowledges that it's a tough course, and not everyone who attempts it is successful. In fact, he added that, in some of the most challenging courses, 50 percent of the students are unsuccessful.

Furthermore, Marquez said his company creates scenarios in which they use simunitions (non-lethal bullets) that add reality to their training scenarios. They teach the students to respond to a real situation and to think and make the right decision. Importantly, he indicated, "We have to change our training to meet the changing tactics of the enemy."

Calling his program a training laboratory, Marquez said his students must be fast and accurate because they are making life-and-death decisions. The Silver Eagle venture is important to the future growth of his company. Marquez wants to make this company a success. If his company could tailor its programs to meet the new threats, he believes it would take them to the next level of growth.

"The challenges we face today are much more daunting," Marquez said, as he reaffirmed the importance of training not only existing law enforcement personnel, but citizens at large who desire to learn to protect themselves through an innovative program. This training laboratory seeks to counter how the adversary is operating, and he said the adversary's behavior is fluid and his tactics are ever-changing. Thus, Marquez said the Silver Eagle Group constantly adapts to the changes of our adversary. Consequently, he said, "Our philosophy is that training is never static, but must constantly evolve." Marquez said the Silver Eagle Group is the most comprehensive and innovative training available anywhere.

Because of Marquez's success as an entrepreneur who understands the dangers to not only the United States but Virginia as well, Timothy Kaine, the former Virginia governor, appointed him to the Virginia Secure Commonwealth Panel in 2008, which oversees the state's homeland security preparedness. Also, Virginia Governor Bob McDonnell has chosen Marquez to his National Security Panel, which consists of leaders from government, the business world, and retired military leaders who will advise the governor on developing the best strategies to retain military and national security facilities located in Virginia and attract new operations and facilities to the state.

Outreach in Education

As a Hispanic, Dario Marquez is keenly interested in outreach and helping as many younger kids as possible in the community. He said, "When I was in a position to do something, it was in my DNA to give back to the community because of what my mother had done for me." Further, he said his mother, whose earnings resulted from working in a factory, was willing to help one of Marquez's friends pay for his entire education if he went to college.

Marquez said, "My goal is primarily supporting organizations that are helping young Latinos and others to get into college." Marquez said he gives financially to education charities and serves as chairman of the Hispanic College Fund (HCF) as well as supporting the Latino Student Fund, the Esperanza Fund, and the Gala Theatre Education Program.

Education and entrepreneurs are inextricably linked, according to Marquez. "Not only do I have a passion for education, but I am also an entrepreneur. The organizations I support not only educate but lift the entrepreneurial spirit."

Dario Marquez has come far in his life. As a young boy, he aspired to become a leader. I am sure that the man in his dreams who walked confidently through the industrial plant and who was his mentor as he sat in his mother's car during his youth in Dover, New Jersey, would be very proud of him because he became a successful entrepreneur. Moreover, and equally important, Marquez's entrepreneurship—the creation of his company, including the presence of the thirty-five hundred employees who staff his global and domestic operations; the services performed by MVM and the Silver Eagle Group that benefit the citizens of the United States; and his outreach endeavors that have enhanced the lives of Hispanic Americans—all of these are manifestations of Adam Smith's invisible hand.

David Ward, Contractor and Voting Machine Entrepreneur

We're exporting democracy to the world.

In ancient Greek mythology, the hero Sisyphus attempted to push a rock to the top of a mountain, only to see it fall to the bottom. Undaunted by the challenge, Sisyphus pushed the rock until it reached the summit. While the rock did not remain at the top, nevertheless, Sisyphus did succeed in reaching his goal.

As his former commercial insurance agent for twenty-five years, I had long seen the late David Ward as a modern-day reincarnation of the mythical Sisyphus. Having taken over a family-owned sewer and water construction company, Ward & Stancil, following the death of his father in 1974, he confronted bankruptcy because of a downturn in construction and a sharp drop in cash receipts following the recession of the early 1970s that OPEC's huge increase in oil prices, in large part, precipitated. Determined to succeed, however, Ward worked out an agreement with two friends, one of whom was a consultant who purchased his company's debt, thereby allowing his construction company to regain its financial strength and focus on growth.

In the aftermath of its return to profitability, Ward repaid the loan that allowed Ward & Stancil to participate in the economic upswing and increase in housing construction that occurred in subdivisions in the Richmond area during the years prior to the housing bust in 2007.

As a contractor who engaged in underground sewer and water

construction for municipalities and general contractors, and unlike many of the entrepreneurs in his industry, Ward had a vital interest in the larger community that transcended the profits that he and his industry earned. Specifically, he wanted the public to view his industry more favorably because a contractor, for example, who severed an underground gas, electrical, water, or sewer facility could cause bodily harm, property damages, and an interruption in vital services to the public. It might also cause irreparable damage to the contractor's reputation.

David Ward Relaxing

Protecting Citizens of Virginia

Because of Ward's interest in relations between the state and his industry, according to Massoud Tahamtani, director of the Division of Utility and Rail Safety for the Virginia State Corporation Commission, the governor of Virginia appointed him to the Board for Contractors, "whose purpose was to establish rules for licensing various types of contractors" in Virginia.

Tahamtani said the Virginia Underground Utility Damage Prevention Act stipulated a member of the Board must serve on the Commission's Damage Prevention Advisory Committee.

Consequently, according to Tahamtani, Ward was chosen by the Board and appointed by the Commission to serve on the Advisory Committee. Once a month, David Ward, Tahamtani, and eleven other members representing utilities, contractors, and the state government met to review damages to underground facilities that excavation activities caused. Specifically, this group reviewed the actions by all persons and companies involved in the damages and decided the appropriate enforcement action. Thus, it could dismiss the case, issue a warning letter, and even assess penalties up to $2,500.

Tahamtani said Ward performed "a fantastic job in taking his contractor hat off and acting in an unbiased manner," which he said was difficult for some to separate their own interest from those of the citizens of Virginia. Moreover, Tahamtani said Ward was probably one of the toughest people on the contractors. In fact, he said the work Ward did brought a lot of credibility to the process. In appreciation of his work with the Advisory Committee and his leadership in advancing Virginia's damage prevention program, he was presented with the Damage Prevention Leadership Award in 2001, the first of its kind in Virginia to be given to an individual. Normally, companies received this award.

Ward & Stancil Sewer Project

In 2002, the SCC allowed the creation of a nonprofit corporation called the Virginia Utility Protection Service (VUPS), which created a new one-call notification center based in Roanoke that required any company or even an individual to notify it prior to any project involving underground excavation. Ward became chairman of VUPS in 2002 and was a member of its board until his death. Tahamtani said he drove to and from Roanoke many times to help get the center's business done.

Voting Machine Entrepreneur

Ward's entrepreneurial skills transcended operations that his underground sewer and water construction company performed. Accordingly, while still president of Ward & Stancil and confident in his ability to lead an entirely different business, he purchased a company in 1981 named International Roll Call (IRC) from a neighbor, Billy Pitts, who continued to work with Ward for several years until his death.

Marshall F. Thompson founded Thompson Voting Machine Company, which was to become IRC, in the 1920s. According to its website, it:

> [R]evolutionized the art of electrical voting in 1942, installing the first high-speed voting systems in the Virginia Senate and House of Delegates … pioneered the use of computer-driven voting systems and the utilization of software programs to enhance efficiency and productivity in the administrative and clerical area of the legislative process.[20]

Ward & Stancil & IRC Main Building

Ward's wife, Debbie, said her husband was "always looking over the next hill because he was a visionary and loved challenges." One close friend said, "David saw business as a game rather than just a dog-eat-dog endeavor where owners become rich."

In his best-selling book, *The Money Game*, Wall Street investor, George J.W. Goodman, who wrote under the pseudonym of Adam Smith, said that some entrepreneurs view business as a game. Money is important, but the real thrill lies in the actual game, a process that consists of the daily challenges of operating a business, negotiating deals, arranging financing for new projects, overcoming hurdles, and realizing success.

Ward majored in mechanical engineering at Virginia Polytechnic Institute (VPI) and understood machines. But to gain a foothold in the industry, in 2001, he purchased the customer base from Daktronics Corporation, which had designed and manufactured voting machines since 1971.

Ward was confident he could turn around IRC and gain market share. But to become better equipped to lead a small electronics company, he completed courses at Radio Shack in which he increased his knowledge of computers and software. His wife said, "The older machines that had defined IRC prior to David's acquisition of the company were electro-mechanical, but they lacked flexibility." Her husband combined the new software that was being developed for computers into a true voting machine that thirty-eight states, many cities in the United States, and a few countries in the Middle East and Latin America use. Three months before his death in 2008, Ward returned from Jordan and Nicaragua, where he had installed voting machines.

As evidence of Ward's innovative skills, the new computerized machines clearly displayed a legislator's decision (a yes or no) whereas the older electro-mechanical devices could only indicate a line or scratch next to the name. All machines are assembled at IRC's headquarters in eastern Hanover County. The proof of Ward's success as head of IRC lay in his ability to boost sales to $5 million before his death from less than $100,000 when he purchased IRC. Ms. Ward said her husband's successful leadership of IRC's voting machines was important to him in a way that transcended profits and personal recognition. "He liked to say, 'What we are doing is exporting democracy to the world.'"

IRC Voting Machine in Virginia Legislature

The Ability to Focus

A few years prior to his death, I had asked Ward about the qualities that defined his ability to become a leader of an enterprise. He said he knew how to focus. His son, David Jr., said he had the capacity to tune out distractions and events around him. I can attest to Ward's ability to concentrate or focus since I was his commercial property and casualty insurance agent for a quarter century and remember many conversations with him about the proper methods to insure the risk in the operations of his business at an affordable cost. Like many entrepreneurs, Ward was concerned about the cost to insure his corporate assets, but he never cut corners because he wanted to be protected.

The significance of being able to focus is crucial to entrepreneurs. In a January 27, 2011 interview with *AOL Jobs Week*, Donald Trump said he wished he had realized the importance of focus in the early nineties. "When I had a financial turnaround in the early 90s, I realized I had lost my focus." This fact led the famous investor to declare Chapter 11 bankruptcy.[21]

Social Outreach

The turnaround in operations at Ward & Stancil and the explosive growth at IRC are only part of the real David Ward. Indeed, the man who rescued Ward & Stancil from near financial death with the help of friends, turbocharged the growth of IRC, and served on a state advisory committee to monitor damages caused by contractors in his own industry also cared deeply about his employees and persons less fortunate than he had been in life.

In fact, Ward was passionate about helping people who lacked food to eat. "He was always on the lookout for someone who needed a helping hand," said his wife. As evidence of his compassion, he made a payroll deduction to the Central Virginia Food Bank each week for the final twenty-two months of his life. His wife said that, in this way, he would not forget to send money to the food bank. During the approximate thirty years that I knew him, I had no idea that he made this type of commitment to help the poor.

Other important qualities defined David Ward. His wife said he always desired to become an entrepreneur because working for someone else was not going to happen to him. He learned frugality and sacrifice as a young boy. For example, he sold real estate, constructed and owned apartments, worked in the motel industry, drove a taxi, and built swimming pools, but failed in the plastics manufacturing business prior to his purchase of IRC.

His mother taught him to be frugal, a quality that marked much of his life when she saved the profits that he made on a paper route. Moreover, at fourteen years of age, she required him to pay for his room and board. Later, when he enrolled in college at VPI, she gave him the money from his earlier paper route to pay for his tuition. He also served his country in the Korean War as a parachute jumper with the 101st Airborne Division of the Army.

In addition to his passion for the food bank, he was CFO for the nonprofit TLC Global Outreach, Inc., an organization that provided help to children. He also had a fondness for horses, as evidenced by his formation of a company named Stillmeadows Farms that maintained horses for riders in the community.

His deep compassion for the poor who lacked adequate food, his role serving the people of Virginia in the close working relationship with the state organization that sought to protect its citizens from cutting sewer and other underground cables by his own company and others as well, and his vision that IRC could ship democracy to other citizens of the world by selling voting machines, these are the important factors that helped define my friend and former client, David Ward, who, like Dario Marquez and the other entrepreneurs in this book, embody Smith's famous invisible hand idea.

Sharon Dabney-Wooldridge,
Janitorial Company Owner

I drove my Nissan 200SX to clean a home.

Sharon Dabney-Wooldridge had no lack of role models in her life: a father who was an owner and operator of two small grocery stores, a grandfather who became the proprietor of a farm, an uncle who was the founder of a dump truck business, a mother and grandmother who worked to clean homes, and a great-uncle who created his frame shop. All of these family members inspired Sharon, a single black mom, to create a janitorial company, KleaneKare Team, Inc., in 1987 and become one of the most successful minority entrepreneurs in the Richmond area.

Prior to the creation of her business, Dabney-Wooldridge worked briefly as a banker at United Virginia Bankshares (now SunTrust Bank) and even attempted to sell investment products before attending Virginia Commonwealth University (VCU). Her experience in banking and investments provided some knowledge for starting a business. However, Dabney-Wooldridge really learned the skills of being an entrepreneur on her own over the past quarter century or, as some may say, by "the school of hard knocks" in a business community that males long dominated.

After attending a few classes at VCU in the mid-1980s, this inspirational lady said, "I would drive my 1986 Nissan 200SX, which contained cleaning materials in the trunk, to clean a home." Coupled with plain hard work and perseverance, this seemingly small event propelled her to create a large company in the ensuing years that grew from two employees in the beginning to one that currently employs one hundred people and generates sales that exceed $4 million.

First Janitorial Contract

Not long after the formation of KleaneKare, Dabney-Wooldridge won her first governmental janitorial or cleaning contract at Fort Lee, the US Army base located about twenty-five miles southeast of Richmond. Working in the headquarters building at Fort Lee was quite overwhelming, she admitted in a January 19, 2011 interview with the Richmond-based publication *Urban Views*.[22]

Over the past quarter century, her customer base has grown to include not only governmental entities but industrial, commercial, and health care companies in the local area. Some of her local customers include Phillip Morris USA, Dominion Resources, Bon Secours—Memorial Regional Medical Center, Virginia Housing Development Authority, Children's Choice Learning Center, Commonwealth Cancer Center, Federal Aviation Administration, Department of Veteran Affairs, Richmond Redevelopment and Housing Authority, Maggie L. Walker Business and Technology Center, Carrier Enterprises, and many other local companies.

Dabney-Wooldridge continues to seek new clients despite her success in retaining KleaneKare's customer base. In fact, her company emerged from the 2008 economic recession remarkably unscathed, having retained most, if not all, of her customers. Not many companies can make this claim. In fact, some smaller companies in her industry have closed. Many of these smaller janitorial firms simply lacked the depth and resources to continue operations. According to a report from Manta.com, there were 2,125 janitorial companies in Virginia in 2010. The online service did not offer a breakdown of the details of the industry in the state.[23]

The janitorial industry is fragmented, an indication that no single company or group of enterprises is dominant. Powerhomebiz. com labels the cleaning industry as consisting of mostly mom-and-pop businesses. IBISworld, a website that produces information on various industries, indicated in a May 28, 2011 report, "After losing revenue due to weak demand from households and businesses during the recession, the industry is set to improve."[24]

According to Hoovers, a Dun & Bradstreet company website, "The U.S. janitorial services and carpet cleaning industry consists of about fifty thousand janitorial companies and about nine thousand carpet and upholstery cleaning companies with combined revenue of about $40 billion."[25]

Sharon Dabney-Wooldridge

The above statistics are included for information purpose only. However, based on the data and Dabney-Wooldridge's proven ability to manage a large company with a diversified customer base, her janitorial company has performed admirably.

Company Philosophy

Importantly, KleaneKare employees embrace a set of common principles or company culture that separates her company from many other janitorial enterprises. These principles are taught in many leading business schools and contained in books of leading writers such as Tom Peters and others. These include:

> Build trust, value others, communicate effectively, drive execution, foster innovation, focus on the customer, collaborate with others, solve problems creatively and demonstrate high integrity, maintain professional internal and external relationships that meet company core values. Proactively establish and maintain effective work team relationships with all support departments.

While practicing a common culture is crucial to building a strong organization, KleaneKare's daily operations require the right team around you, as Dabney-Wooldridge indicated.

Learning these basic and important principles is part of KleaneKare's training program that also includes compliance with OSHA regulations and safety measures that protect employees from accidents that not only may result in bodily injuries and lost time but also drive workers' compensation insurance costs higher and impair efficiencies.

Combined with the principles that comprise the company culture, KleaneKare is committed to what it terms core values or a TEAM motto that means, "Together Everyone Achieves More," a concept that is critical to growth and the retention of customers.

Being a leader in janitorial services is important to KleaneKare. In fact, its website refers to what it labels as "sick building symptoms," conditions that result from neglect or improper building maintenance. These include irritation in the eyes, nose and throat that are marked by pain, dryness, stinging, hoarseness and voice problems, skin irritation, headaches, sluggishness, mental and physical fatigue, memory loss and a difficulty in focusing, and hypersensitivity, such as a runny nose, teary eyes, and asthma-like conditions. It is easy to shrug off these issues, but they can hinder a company's productivity and result in higher costs.

Innovation is very important to the success of KleaneKare. Unlike some smaller competitors, KleaneKare has fully embraced green technological products, or what is called the "GreenKleane Program" with a passion. Using new products that promote a clean and safe environment are very important to the customers of KleaneKare. For example, its employees use innovative products such as a vacuum backpack that enables them to clean areas faster and more efficiently than, say, using the traditional stand-alone vacuum cleaner that Hoover introduced years ago. Also important to the cleaning process is a microfiber cloth and ergonomic mops, products that help ensure a cleaner and greener environment for KleaneCare's customers.

Prior to a new relationship with a customer, KleaneKare performs what Dabney-Wooldridge calls a site inspection. Referred to as the KleaneKare Audit, this process enables her employees to be aware of all areas to be cleaned as well as offer possible recommendations to the customer. Importantly, this audit process is repeated regularly to ensure KleaneKare's employees are fulfilling their obligation to the customer. All new employees are schooled in the importance and proper methods of janitorial work. Thus, a training program is required for new employees who are taught the importance of providing the best service to the customer.

In addition to the audit process described previously and the GreenKleane Program, KleaneKare offers the Quick Staff Process that enables the company to present the best qualified and most efficient staff for special work requirements, as opposed to some regular cleaning requirements. Finally it offers a FlexKleane Policy that grants her workers the authority to engage in certain cleaning tasks that could lie outside of the normal scope of operations.

Customer and Employee Satisfaction

Dabney-Wooldridge understands the critical importance of customer satisfaction. For example, she related one story in which she described a customer who called to report that there was no toilet paper after the KleaneKare janitorial employee completed the job and left the premises. "I delivered the toilet paper myself since everyone was busy," she said. Dabney-Wooldridge stated her quick response is very important to not only her company, but to customer retention as well.

While a satisfied customer is very important to KleaneKare, Dabney-Wooldridge is quick to praise her employees because she believes in "the importance of having a staff that is on board with taking the company to the next level." To reach this new level, she stressed the importance of loyalty, commitment, professionalism, positive attitude, dedication, and just all-around ownership of the company vision.

Dabney-Wooldridge does not live a flamboyant lifestyle, preferring modesty instead. Family and friends are very important to her. Also, faith is very significant as well to her, a process she reaffirms through her membership at St. Paul's Baptist Church, where the highly acclaimed and inspirational minister, Lance Watson, preaches.

KleaneKare has won awards that are indicative of its success:

- Micro Enterprise Merit Award from Virginia Microenterprise Network (2000)

- Image Awards from the Building Service Contractors Association International (2003)

- Entrepreneur of the Year from the Metro and Business League of Richmond (2006)

- RideFindersGreen Partner Award (2010)

Dabney-Wooldridge was also a featured speaker at the Women's Entrepreneur Convention at the Convention Center in Richmond in late January 2011.

Determined to continue her success and help other people in the process, Dabney-Wooldridge knows who she is, where she came from, and where she is going in life. Her son, Farley, who has served his country as a gunnery sergeant in the US Marine Corps for ten years, plans to work with his mom in her company when he retires from the military in about ten to twelve years. He hopes to help his mother continue her success as an entrepreneur and in which both of them will continue to generate benefits to not only KleaneKare but to the entire community.

When she drove her 1986 Nissan to clean homes about twenty-five years ago, it is doubtful that Dabney-Wooldridge foresaw that she would lead a large business venture in the Richmond area. But it is clear to me that the reasons for her success lie in her decision to embrace innovation and environmentally friendly equipment and materials, as well as create an atmosphere that is very supportive of her employees who consistently demonstrate superior service to KleaneKare's customers.

Patrick Duffeler Sr., Winery Owner

Life is made up of emotions.

In the aftermath of Anheuser-Busch's construction of its beer manufacturing plant and popular theme park in Williamsburg, Virginia, in 1975, some local wine lovers expressed a desire for a world-class winery in the former colonial city.

Eight years later in 1983, Williamsburg wine connoisseurs got their wish when entrepreneur Patrick Duffeler Sr. purchased a nearby historic 320-acre farm, named it Wessex Hundred, and built the Williamsburg Winery, which was to become the largest of its kind in the state of Virginia. In 1985, Duffeler planted the first field of Chardonnay vines for his new venture. Two years later, his company crushed its first Virginia grapes, a process that led to its first award in 1988 when the very popular Governor White brand won a gold medal a few weeks after it was released for sale. In the ensuing years, Williamsburg Winery's wines routinely have been voted among the Best Wines of the World by the coveted Decanter World Wine Awards of London.

The Williamsburg winery's manufacturing facility, which produces nearly sixty thousand cases annually and employs up to eighty people at peak season in the summer and fall, has generated positive benefits for the surrounding area, as evidenced by the creation of new jobs, higher tax revenue for the city of Williamsburg and neighboring James City County, and the beckoning of tourists to the historic area.

European Entrepreneurial Experience

Prior to founding the Williamsburg Winery, Duffeler, who was born in Brussels and received his bachelor of science degree in economics and finance at the University of Rochester, also worked for one of the largest international companies, Eastman Kodak, before jetting to Lausanne, Switzerland, where he became director of marketing for Philip Morris Europe.

During his business career with the European subsidiary of the U.S. tobacco giant, he was chosen to head Philip Morris' famed Formula 1 motor racing group known as the Marlboro World Championship Team. Many of his tasks as head of the Marlboro team included racing safety, working with racetrack organizers, and attracting more sponsors to the sport, tasks he absolutely enjoyed and which he said absorbed him. Importantly, Duffeler's Marlboro Formula 1 team won the world championship in racing in 1974. He also led a team to the Grand Prix in Brazil in the same year.

right to left: Patrick Duffeler Sr. and Jr.

Duffeler's nearly fourteen years in Europe included not only his position with Philip Morris. Importantly, he also gained a tremendous knowledge of the wine industry in Burgundy, France, which he would apply later at his own winery in colonial Williamsburg. In the early 1980s, Duffeler was named president of Fragrances Selective in New York City with headquarters in Geneva, Switzerland, and Barcelona, Spain.

His contacts with wine connoisseurs on the European continent, combined with his positions with Philip Morris, Formula 1, and Fragrances Selective, provided invaluable knowledge for his own venture as an entrepreneur in the winery business in Williamsburg, Virginia. He said his investment in winemaking was based on the following factors:

- The wine industry is very fragmented, as evidenced, for example, by some one hundred and seventy-five wineries in the state of Virginia alone.

- There is an ease of entry into the industry, a factor that encourages both small and large entrepreneurs to enter winemaking.

- The cost of advertising is low. There is a lot of consumer interest in wine, and the quality of the product itself is very important. Also contributing to the low advertising expenses of wineries such as the Williamsburg Winery are the two hundred and fifty awards it has gained over its more than a quarter-century history.

Factors That Led to Success

Like any competent and knowledgeable entrepreneur, Duffeler, who received *INC* magazine's Entrepreneur of the Year award in 1997, understands the important factors that have led to the success of his company. These include taking care of his employees and providing good benefits to them, and, very importantly, delivering a superior product to his customers that appeals to their imagination or senses. Duffeler, an engaging and intelligent man, learned that some large companies allocate millions of dollars to research and development to create complex and sophisticated technological products, but forget that the senses and emotions are critically important to closing the sale. He said, "Life is made up of emotions and how we humans feel about something." He also said he has no respect for companies that make products in which the packaging costs more than the actual product, a statement which lends support to author David Croslin's argument when he said that simplicity, time, and money were the most important factors to generating sales in a company.[26]

Vineyards in Early Spring

As this book has demonstrated, entrepreneurs must innovate to grow their businesses. In this connection, the Williamsburg Winery is no exception, albeit, its implementation of new ideas differs radically from, say, a high-technology company. According to Patrick Duffeler Jr., the development of its largest-selling wine, the aforementioned Governor White brand, was innovative in that it was named after Virginia's first governor, William Berkeley, and is responsible for spurring growth in the company and landing it at the top of all wineries in the state of Virginia. Also contributing to his company's success is an impressive manufacturing facility located on the premises.

In addition to providing a boost to the local economy, the land that the Williamsburg Winery occupies is rich in history. According to the winery's website, the Hundred name refers to parcels of land sufficient to support a hundred families regardless of acreage in the early seventeenth century. Moreover, the land was said to be governed by the Twelfth Acte of the House of Burgesses in 1619, which mandated that each colonial settler must plant at least ten vines for the purpose of making wine on his land.

Management Team

Fortunately, a team of strong managers who bring many commendable skills to its operations and leadership surround the Williamsburg Winery. In addition to its founder, Patrick Duffeler Sr., his son, Patrick Duffeler Jr., who graduated from the College of William and Mary with a degree in American history, was born in Switzerland and lived much of his youth on the European continent. He is chief operating officer at the winery. Six years before his arrival in Virginia, he learned much about the winery business, including his attendance at winery management classes at University of California Davis and while working as an intern at a winery in Bordeaux in France. As vice president and manager of planning at the Williamsburg Winery, he coordinates the operational aspects of the winery.

Vice President Matthew G.R. Meyer, a very able and knowledgeable man who was born in Great Britain and learned to appreciate wine during his many journeys around the world, heads the Williamsburg Winery's actual winemaking or oenology operations. Meyer also attended the highly esteemed wine school, University of California Davis, where he completed two degrees, one being in oenology and viticulture (producing grapes) and a minor in business and marketing.

The Winemaking Process

Prior to the actual manufacturing of wine, the process of viticulture, which is defined as the science, production, and study of grapes and is a branch of horticulture, must occur. At the Williamsburg Winery, Tom Child, the vineyard manager whose more than three decades of experience is manifest in the production of premium wine grapes, heads the process of viticulture. Importantly, his experience lies in grape nursery operations, crop production, and the economies of agricultural land development and modification to the Williamsburg Winery. He earned his bachelor of science degree in agriculture management and served on the board of the California Rootstock Improvement Commission. He is a member of the American Society for Enology and Viticulture.

Wine Shop

The process of winemaking, whose historical roots extend back some estimated eight thousand years, generally includes harvesting, fermentation, crushing, and destemming, all of which occur on the premises of the Williamsburg Winery. In the late spring and early summer, the actual berries are visible as they ripen on the vines. The harvesting process, in which grapes are removed from the vines, begins in September. Guests can observe some of the manufacturing process at Wessex Hall, which contains the machinery that manufactures the finished product and the large oak barrels that store wine.

Connoisseurs of wine and visitors to the Williamsburg Winery's more than fifty acres of property can purchase products in its popular wine shop, which feature several varieties of grapes, consisting of Merlot, Cabernet Franc, Petite Verdot, and the aforementioned very popular Governor White wine. The Williamsburg Winery is the largest of its kind in Virginia, producing an estimated 20 percent of all wine in the state on its fifty beautiful acres of vineyards about ten minutes from colonial Williamsburg and not far from the historic James River and Jamestown, the first colonial settlement in America in 1607.

Lunch at Gabriel Archer Tavern

The grounds and buildings of Wessex Hundred reflect the architecture and motif of both the Old World and Colonial Williamsburg. For example, near the building that houses the winemaking facility, visitors can enjoy meals and wines at the Williamsburg Winery's highly acclaimed Gabriel Archer Tavern, named after an English-born gentleman who came to Virginia in the early seventeenth century and was co-captain of the ship, *Godspeed*, which transported early colonial settlers from England to Jamestown. This tavern features excellent lunches and dinners and relaxing views of the vineyards and acres of the local countryside. One of its popular-selling wines, Gabriel Archer Reserve, is named after this seventeenth-century English settler.

Located on the same property and only a hundred or so yards from the Gabriel Archer Tavern, visitors can relax at the Wedmore Place, a country hotel that features twenty-eight bedrooms and suites named after several well-known provinces on the European continent. Thus, for example, visitors have their choices of the Scandinavia Room, the sitting room of the Venetian Suite, the Vienna Room, the Lombardi Room, and other similar rooms. The Williamsburg Winery provides a perfect setting for weddings and other catered events at Wessex Hall, Susan Constant Hall, and Reserve Cellar, which is surrounded by shelves of wine bottles.

Wine Tasting Shop

Operating a first-class winery has been a rewarding experience for

Duffeler. However, it has not always been easy for him. Despite his overall success as an entrepreneur, he said, "I have gotten my hands dirty and even scrubbed the restroom floors on my knees when I had to do it." Moreover, like other business owners profiled in this book, he has had setbacks, with the weather providing the worst of them. A few years ago, his winery lost a sizeable portion of its grapes from a hailstorm. Coupled with gasoline prices per gallon that exceeded $4 per gallon in 2008 and reached nearly the same amount in the spring of 2011, some events are beyond his control. However, as long as the Duffeler family is in control of the Williamsburg Winery, wine lovers can expect to be served superior products and hospitality in an atmosphere that reflects the very best of the Old and New Worlds. Equally important, Duffeler's company should continue to generate benefits for not only its customers and employees, but the entire community as well.

Mark Motley, Auctioneer

*Our goal has been to maximize
our customers' opportunities.*

If you mention the word "auction," some people may conjure up a fast-talking auctioneer who screams out prices to a group of anxious buyers and sellers. To Mark Motley, auctions have been a way of life since he was thirteen when his father, who founded Motley's Auction in 1967, allowed him to participate in the process of auctioning antiques. It was not until the late 1980s, however, that Motley, who attended Virginia Commonwealth University, took over the business after his mother's death and built it into a large and highly respected diversified auction company with annual sales over $50 million.

The remarkable growth under the leadership of Motley tracks the upswing in the entire auction industry. According to an online report from the National Auctioneers Association (NAA), live auction industry revenue in 2007 grew 5.3 percent to $270.7 billion over the prior year, the most recent date of the report. The survey measures live auctions only, thereby excluding online auctions where growth is rapidly growing.[27]

According to the NAA report, residential real estate outpaced other types of auctions, a fact that is not surprising, owing to the housing boom that occurred from the 1990s until it came to a screeching halt in late 2007 and early 2008. Automobile auctions represented the second-largest single specialty category of auctions after residential housing, according to the NAA report. While commercial and industrial machinery and equipment ranked third, other leading segments within the auction industry included land and agricultural real estate, commercial and industrial real estate, and charity art, antiques, collectibles, and other miscellaneous groups.

History of Auctioneering

Historians agree that the first auctions occurred as early as 500 BC when the ancient Greek leader, Herodutus, sold women on the condition that they were married.[28] Auctions were used more extensively during the Roman Empire when slaves were auctioned and maintained their popularity during the early modern world of the seventeenth and eighteenth centuries when they occurred in European taverns and coffee houses. Also during this period of time, well-established and upscale firms such as Sotheby's and Christie's were founded. There are many different types of auctions, including English, the Dutch sealed bid, the Vickrey, and many other types.

CEO, Mark Motley

In fact, auctions were manifest in early American history in which furs, tobacco, corn, and other necessities were accepted items in this process. The online site, auctiontecs.com, says:

> Most pieces of machinery go through an auction
> several times in their useful life ... When an industrial
> facility or commercial facility closes down or moves,
> an auction is almost always involved.[29]

Auto Auctions

Motley's Auctions has made significant progress following Mark Motley's control of the company in 1987. While antiques are still part of the company's product line, today, Motley's engages in public and online auctions of automobiles, industrial products and real estate, recreational vehicles, motorcycles, boats, antiques, and other products. Appraisals are also included.

Motley's Auto Auction began in 1989 and boasts a clientele that includes banks, finance companies, governmental agencies, fleets, and both new and used car dealerships throughout the state of Virginia. These auto auctions, which comprise the company's second-highest group of sales after real estate, occur on Friday mornings at the company's large open lot facility four miles south of downtown Richmond on Interstate 95. Here, fast-talking auctioneers attempt to sell cars to buyers who gather inside a large garage that contains two lanes of cars that move forward as they chant a rhythmic flow of numbers. A typical sequence of words during a live auto auction may go as follows, "$2,000 bid, now two, now two, will you give me two." Professional auctioneers speak in rapid-fire fashion to create excitement among the crowds gathered around them. These guys are full of adrenalin.

Motley's Main Location

Prior to its entry into auto auctions, Motley's desired to gain credibility before launching a more diversified product line. Thus, in 1988, Motley won contracts to sell surplus equipment for the city of Richmond, power equipment for Virginia Power Company (now Dominion Virginia Power), and industrial equipment for the blue-chip companies of Philip Morris (now Altria) and Reynolds Metals (purchased by Alcoa).

"We wanted to demonstrate that we were able to handle transactions and large items for highly respected government and corporate entities," said Motley when asked the significance of these transactions.

Armed with more experience from these larger entities, Motley's began to feature many industrial equipment items used for construction and manufacturing and technology that are also auctioned at the Deepwater Terminal site. Occasionally, Motley even auctions small corporate aircraft.

Motley's is structured to provide impartial professional certified appraisals for estate planning and settlement, tax and insurance management, and commercial financing. Motley's brochure on professional certified appraisals claims, "Our goal is to assign values to your objects that accurately reflect their value in the current marketplace."

Some people may be under the erroneous impression that only technology companies engage in innovation. In recent years, Motley said he has elevated the auction experience into different categories featured by his company. Thus, a manager heads each main product line: autos, antiques and appraisals, real estate, and industrial products. In this way, the particular specialty division receives the attention and focus of a qualified professional appraiser.

A second example of positive change that Motley embraced was the move of the auto auction from property in eastern Henrico County near the airport to the much larger and more visible location at Deepwater Terminal that is located south of the city of Richmond. Thus, most of the company's sales are generated at one highly recognizable location. Also, Motley sends employees to certified auction schools to enhance and expand their knowledge as well as sharpen their skills.

To create more growth for his company, Motley has occasionally gone against advice that turned out to be wrong. For example, many people told him to schedule auctions on weekends only. They laughed when he decided to hold auctions during the days of the week and real estate auctions even at night, with some of them telling him that no one would come to auctions held during the week. They were wrong. The auto auction occurs each Friday at 10:00 a.m., and other auctions occur at night and different weekdays. He turned down the idea to schedule his auctions on weekends because many people engage in family or leisure time activities, events that would detract and even be counterproductive to his business.

A Motley Billboard

Riding a wave of success for himself and his employees in which his company has become a highly regarded business venture, Motley, a high-energy and compassionate entrepreneur, has enjoyed the journey. Like some other business owners, Motley did not start the business, but he did infuse its growth and move it to much higher levels of success. However, he is quick to point out that complacency is very dangerous. "I often look over my shoulder because a competitor can gain ground fast and we could make a mistake." For example, Motley made the mistake of embracing the Internet as a way in which to conduct auctions too early.

Intuitively, his belief that auctions could be conducted online was not wrong. But his mistake lay only in the timing of the venture and not its idea. So Motley and his associates, Bill Fischer and John Montgomery, began the online process just before the dot-com bubble burst in the late 1990s, thereby destroying the hopes of many businesses as well as Motley's online venture. Fortunately, it was not a costly decision. Rather, the problem was that he was too early because now his company generates over half of all sales online on a profitable basis, and he believes online transactions will continue to comprise a larger share of his business in the future. Although unable to secure much-needed funding in the beginning for Motley's online auction venture, he went head-to-head with well-established juggernauts such as Amazon.com and eBay, and *Computer* magazine recognized it as a Top 500 website on the Internet, an enviable accomplishment.

Focus on Employees and Customers

Motley enjoys being surrounded by many wonderful employees, all of whom work very hard. In a paid advertisement on April 30, 2007 in the *Richmond Times-Dispatch,* Motley wrote that the success of his auction business was not because of him. Rather, he said it lay with the staff, because:

Motley's has been gifted with over sixty-five full- and part-time professionals who are some of the brightest, most dedicated, and hardest working team players bar-none. They are put in difficult circumstances regularly and always rise to the occasion to best serve our customers.[30]

The second reason for his company's success is his customers, who are critical to any business venture. He said:

> I have been honored to work for some of the greatest and most fascinating people in the world, many of whom have entrusted Motley's to sell their entire life savings … Many of our customers today were at the auction the first night I started my auction career some thirty-four years ago.

He elaborated further on the significance of his clients in his Richmond Auto Auction brochure in which he wrote that he understands completely that his company's operations are inextricably tied to the future of his customers. In fact, he said, "We operate with the belief that our success can only be realized if our clients succeed …

Therefore, our goal has been to maximize our client's opportunities when remarketing assets."

A Live Motley Auto Auction

But his success would not have occurred without his parents. "They were the true masters of the going-going-gone auction process." He added:

> My parents were the hardest-working people I have
> ever known ... In 1973, my parents put up everything
> they owned to buy the Wigwam (the company's first
> location about ten miles north of Richmond on US
> 1 highway).

His parents taught Motley to embrace what he calls two simple philosophies: treat people honestly and roll out the carpet for everyone.

Community Outreach

The book's introduction, including some of the individual chapters, mentions entrepreneurs who give some of their income back to their communities. Motley is no exception. He has been conducting charity/benefit auctions since he was eighteen years old. These include the American Heart Association, Richmond Ballet, Juvenile Diabetes Research Foundation, Safari Club International, March of Dimes, Ducks Unlimited, and other worthy organizations. He has conducted as many as twenty-three charity events in one year, in not only Virginia, but other states across the nation as well.

The Future

One can expect online auctions to continue their fast growth, owing to the growing popularity of the Internet and the speed with which this process occurs. Still, I seriously doubt that the traditional auction, consisting of sellers and potential buyers gathered together amidst products to be sold where the auctioneer screams out "going, going, gone" will disappear. In fact, there is no reason that both cannot coexist together. But no matter which method of auctioneering is the most popular in the future, one should expect entrepreneur and risk taker, Mark Motley, to remain engaged in this age-old and exciting process.

Despite a few minor mistakes, Motley, like other entrepreneurs in this book, is the consummate risk taker who has embraced innovation, entered new markets, and taken his company to new heights, which would not been accomplished if he had not embraced change. He also personifies Adam Smith's famous invisible hand concept as well one of Art Laffer and Steve Moore's conclusions in their book, *Return to Prosperity: How America Can Regain its Superpower Status*, where they wrote, "Entrepreneurs not only carry other people with them as investors in their journey … They also provide meaningful jobs and high-quality products at low cost."[31]

Bobby Ukrop, Food Company President

Our philosophy is to know, understand, and live the Golden Rule.

After he and his seventy-three-year-old brother, Jim, sold their very popular twenty-five-store supermarket chain in Richmond (with one store in Williamsburg) in early 2010 to the Giant-Carlisle division of Dutch-based conglomerate Ahold following the worst financial recession since 1932, some might have thought that Bobby Ukrop would have given no thought to starting a new career. They would be wrong. In fact, this sixty-four-year-old, high-energy entrepreneur, who graduated from the University of Richmond and the Darden School of Business at the University of Virginia, and his two sons-in-law, Scott Aronson and Chris Kantner, started another company in the food industry in 2010 named Ukrop's Homestyle Foods, which manufactures the same seven hundred items that were sold in Ukrop's Super Markets, Inc., prior to its sale. Bobby Ukrop is president of the new company.

These items (baked at the Ukrop's Bakery in Henrico County) include cakes, cookies, pastries, and other bakery items offered since the acquisition of the former Richmond-based Dot's Pastry Shop in 1976. Also included are other entrees, such as side dishes, sandwiches, salads, cut fruit, vegetable items, and soups that have been cooked and prepared at Ukrop's Kitchen in Chesterfield County since 1989. Even though Ukrop's produced and sold its line of homemade, chilled prepared foods to meet the nutritional and convenience needs of modern families since 1989, only a very limited number of food manufacturers engage in the type of business of Ukrop's Homestyle Foods.

Bobby Ukrop and his brother, Jim, the former chairman of the board of Ukrop's Super Markets, Inc., and chairman of the First Market Bank (now Union First Market Bank) from 1997 to 2010, were always striving to offer their customers high-quality, fresh products. Unfortunately, that proved to be quite a challenge when Ukrop's opened its first in-store bakery in 1971. Since the Ukrops had difficulty locating or making top-notch baked goods, Jim Ukrop approached both Dot's Pastry Shop and Thalhimer's Bakery. However, both companies declined and told him that they were unable to produce any additional food items.

The Purchase of Dot's Pastry Shop

For several years, the in-store bakeries at Ukrop's were mediocre at best. However, two days before Christmas in 1975, Bobby's wife, Jayne, visited Dot's Pastry Shop, and Dot Robinson's husband, Charlie, approached Jayne and said they might want to sell the business because they were nearing retirement and had no children. According to the old adage of "timing is everything," Jayne was at the right place at the right time. On Christmas Eve, Bobby Ukrop went to Dot's to discuss possibilities of a sale with the Robinsons. The Ukrop family had a big discussion of this topic over Christmas dinner. Accordingly, Ukrop's Super Markets, Inc., purchased Dot's during the following year.

Left to right: Scott Aronson, Bobby Ukrop, and Chris Kantner

Known as one of Richmond's best, if not, the best bakery shop, Dot's Pastry Shop was a welcome addition to the Ukrop's organization. Ukrop said, "Our initial goal was that, in five years, customers would say that the baked goods from Dot's (available in all Ukrop's by then) tasted just as delicious as they did when the products were made at the Cary Court pastry shop." In fact, Ukrop's moved bakery production from the original Dot's location on West Cary Street location to what had been the Rolling Pin in the Lakeside section of Richmond and then to its bakery production facility on Southlake Court in Chesterfield County in 1981. Since 1996, Ukrop's baked goods have been produced at Ukrop's Westmoreland Street bakery in Richmond.

By 1981, there were eleven retail stores, and the volume of baked food products had grown tenfold. Ukrop said:

> From 1976 to the late 1980s, we developed confidence in our ability to make the baked goods one day and ship it overnight to be purchased by the customer the following day in our stores. Freshness

and consistency of product were paramount. We did
this in a well-thought-out and controlled manner.

Innovative Kitchen Concept

Similarly, Ukrop said, "Our company made an innovative decision
to embrace the central kitchen concept to produce fresh, chilled
prepared foods that would only require microwave heating." The
idea for Ukrop's central food preparation business came from visits to
retailers in England where third-party producers had long engaged in
making sandwiches, soups, and chilled prepared foods called "ready
meals." With American consumers' lives becoming busier and more
fast-paced, there was a corresponding interest in saving time in the
kitchen. Therefore, the Ukrop brothers thought a central kitchen that
produced this type of food products for their stores (all within an hour
of their plant) would improve consistency, food safety, and freshness.
In describing this innovative idea, Ukrop said, "Given what we had
learned about distribution from our central bakery operation, we felt
we could do the same for chilled prepared foods, 'make today, ship
tonight, and sell tomorrow.'"

The production of top-quality, chilled prepared foods from a
central kitchen became an integral ingredient of a significant presence
of food service in the stores. With a wide array of fresh food offerings
and seating (ranging from seventy-five to one hundred and fifty),
people could eat breakfast, lunch, and dinner at Ukrop's. This in-store
setting served not only its regular store customers but individuals
whose offices were located within walking or short driving distances
of its stores. These customers had been accustomed to patronizing
Ukrop's very popular salad bar since 1984.

Because of the superior quality of its food products and superior
service to customers, Ukrop's was ranked number one in market share
for twenty-two consecutive years (1986–2007) among all Richmond
area grocery store chains. Ukrop, whose company currently employs

approximately five hundred associates, as compared to the six thousand who worked for Ukrop's Super Markets, Inc., in its heyday, intends Ukrop's Homestyle Foods to maintain the same high level of service and attention to its customers and associates as his family did in the past.

Ukrop said that, before its sale in 2009, Ukrop's sold a small amount (less than 10 percent) of its baked goods to a few other grocery chains, including Harris Teeter, Fresh Market, Giant Eagle, Kroger, and Publix. All of these other stores marketed Ukrop's goods under their own label. Ukrop said, "Selling externally was not our focus because serving the customers of our retail stores (including making food for them) was our priority."

Since the family no longer operates a chain of retail food stores, the new business is a food manufacturer with Martin's as its largest customer and Ukrop's Homestyle Foods as Martin's largest supplier in Virginia. The food sold to Martin's is labeled Ukrop's, just as it was before. However, food products shipped outside of Richmond and Williamsburg are sold as Good Meadow Homemades, the name that represents the English version of Dobra Niva, the former Czechoslovakian village where the Ukrop's grandparents lived.

Currently, the Good Meadow products include the famous Ukrop's white house rolls and rainbow cookies sold at Kroger stores in southwest Virginia and Raleigh, North Carolina, and a few stores in West Virginia, Kentucky, and Ohio. Also, a select group of chilled prepared foods, including the very popular chicken salad, was introduced recently to Kroger stores in the Roanoke area. In addition, Ukrop's Homestyle Foods sells several baked goods in the states of Pennsylvania, New Jersey, New York, and Ohio.

Ukrop said that conversations about starting the new business began prior to the sale of the chain in 2010. "Our main focus was taking care of our Richmond customers, many of whom were very loyal to Ukrop's stores. We believe there is a niche for our new business outside of Richmond as well."

Many friends who purchased groceries at the Ukrop's stores over the years were distraught at the sale of this highly respected local institution, so Ukrop's decision to maintain a food presence in Richmond was a relief to many longtime customers.

Company Culture

Like many successful entrepreneurs, the Ukrop brothers experienced several unsuccessful ventures during their long careers. For example, their downtown Richmond ventures—an eatery in the financial district called Fresh Express and a Ukrop's Super Market near Virginia Commonwealth University—did not work out. While Fresh Express operated a satisfactory breakfast business and a very brisk lunch trade, the anticipated take-home dinner business never materialized. Similarly, Joe's Market in Richmond's west end was unprofitable. Ukrop also said the first attempt to make and sell fried chicken in 1971 failed. However, it was reintroduced twelve years later and became a big success.

Like many other entrepreneurs, Ukrop is quick to praise not only his revered customers, but his associates, many of whom were deeply loyal. Now in his new capacity, he is equally serious about his associates. Prior to the sale of Ukrop's Super Markets, Inc., he and his brother gave full-time associates the day off for their birthdays and sent each one a birthday card containing a $50 check. Ukrop still sends birthday cards, arranges a company picnic, and even gives personalized birthday cakes, and he said they seek to create a positive culture within the company. He also described his role as "helping our associates maintain the culture that was created at Ukrop's." Accordingly, he added, "We are striving to maintain the cultural traditions, including encouraging families to spend more time around the table," a worthy endeavor in this fast-paced age when many of us sit longer in front of the computer than eating meals with our family members.

Richmond Sports Backers and Outreach

The Ukrop name has long been associated with good food for many years since the Ukrop's parents opened their first store in 1937 during the Great Depression. Also noteworthy, however, is the family's link to local sports and community outreach, endeavors in which many Ukrop family members are fully engaged. Bobby Ukrop is a co-founder and current president-elect of the Richmond Sports Backers, an organization that owns, manages, or partners with forty different sporting events in the local metropolitan area. According to its website, these events draw nearly 328,000 attendees and help stimulate the local community. Moreover, these events and programs "strengthen the local economy, provide health benefits to participants, and make the region a better place to live." In fact, in a recent CDC study, the Richmond metropolitan area was ranked as one of the most physically active regions in the nation among regions with populations of one million or more. Ukrop said it is also in the nation's top five overall and number one east of the Mississippi.

Among the popular events organized by Sports Backers, a 501(c)(3) charitable nonprofit organization founded in 1991, are the Ukrop's Monument Avenue 10K presented by Martin's, the fourth-largest event of its type in the nation, and the SunTrust Richmond Marathon, the twenty-seventh largest marathon event in the nation. It has also purchased $500,000 of portable sports flooring and equipment to convert the Greater Richmond Convention Center into a sports tournament center. It is little wonder that the National Association of Sports Commissions (NASC) named Sports Backers the best sports commission in the United States in three of the past five years (2006, 2009, and 2011).

Prior to its sale, Ukrop's Super Markets, Inc., gave a minimum of 10 percent of its pre-tax profits to charitable organizations within the community. It also sponsored the Ukrop's/Super Valu Christmas Parade on Broad Street in Richmond. Ukrop said Ukrop's Homestyle

Foods intends to contribute to community outreach events and support charitable organizations including the Central Virginia Foodbank and United Way. The tagline on Bobby's "Ukrop's Homestyle Foods" business card says, "Nourishing families and communities since 1937." On the back of his business card are the words that help define his business, "Our PURPOSE is to nourish lives by sharing our passion for food and families ... Our philosophy is to know, understand, and live the Golden Rule."

Ukrop is also a man of deep faith, as evidenced by his decision to teach a fifth-grade Sunday school class, a commitment he has embraced with great enthusiasm for the past thirty years.

Facts on Employees

In the meantime, Ukrop is fortunate to have a team of skilled and customer-driven individuals to carry on the great tradition of making and delivering delicious and nutritious food. In fact, the veteran, innovative leadership of Ukrop's Homestyle Foods is underpinned by the one hundred and forty-two combined years of experience of the following employees who previously worked for Ukrop's Super Markets, Inc.:

Ten years	Scott Aronson, vice president, business strategy and marketing
Twenty-two years	Glenn Cobb, general manager, Ukrop's Homestyle Foods Bakery
Twenty-two years	Pam Grafton, general manager, Ukrop's Homestyle Foods Kitchen
Eighteen years	Chris Kantner, vice president, production
Twelve years	Gary Larson, vice president, manufacturing
Eight years	Susan Rowe, customer service manager
Twenty-two years	Jason Woodcock, customer relations manager
Twenty-eight years	John Zeheb, vice president, finance

In addition, Ukrop's new company's culinary talent consists of nearly one hundred years of Ukrop's experience as well, as evidenced by the following outstanding employees:

Thomas Pearce, Executive Chef

Pearce has spent more than twenty-five years in the food industry. He trained at the Culinary Institute of America in Hyde Park, New York, and then worked at a five-star French restaurant in Cincinnati, Ohio. Pearce draws on his classic French training for all the recipes he develops for Ukrop's. He also oversees quality control in Ukrop's central kitchen.

Jim Goodman, Executive Pastry Chef

Goodman's passion for pastries began when he was assigned the role of baker in the marines. Goodman's relationship with Ukrop's began even earlier when he worked as a courtesy clerk at the Staples Mill location while he was in high school. Once he was honorably discharged from the marines, Goodman returned to work for Ukrop's as a delivery driver for Dot's Pastry Shop in 1980 and has worked in almost every aspect of Ukrop's Bakery. Goodman obviously has the experience to prove his expertise, but his passion for creating custom cakes makes him stand above the rest. He has won gold and silver medals in national pastry arts competitions; made car-shaped cakes for NASCAR drivers including Mark Martin, Terry Labonte, Jonny Benson, and Greg Sacks; decorated the inaugural cake and several birthday cakes for former Virginia Governor George Allen; and provided cakes for many other prestigious events.

Buntith Chhuon, Certified Pastry Chef

When Chhuon took a part-time high school job working for Chef Otto Bernet's pastry shop, he had no idea it would lead him down a cake-designing career path. He was working as an electrician when he decided he'd rather be in the kitchen. Chhuon got a culinary degree from Richmond Technical Center and eventually became a certified pastry chef. After working at the Jefferson, Chhuon came to work at Ukrop's with Bernet in 1991. His favorite part of making custom cakes is mastering new techniques. "I try to teach myself something every day. I love designing cakes."

Julie Bishop, Manager of Product Development and Quality

As the manager of product development and quality for Ukrop's Homestyle Foods, Bishop works closely with the development chefs and combines her passion for great food with the science and technology behind it to ensure Ukrop's Homestyle Foods meets exceptional quality standards. She graduated magna cum laude from Indiana University of Pennsylvania with a bachelor of science in food and nutrition science and a minor in chemistry and received a master of science degree in food science and technology from Virginia Tech. She has been with Ukrop's since 1993.

Patrick Hadden, Manager of Food Safety

Hadden has devoted his entire career focusing on the maintenance of safe food. He came to Ukrop's in 1995 after working as a consultant and microbiology laboratory manager for a major laboratory that served the entire food industry. Hadden worked with a variety of food industry and government clients, both manufacturers and retailers, in the United States and abroad. As manager of food safety, he uses his broad technical background to keep Ukrop's food fresh, safe, and clean. He also focuses on food safety and security, sanitation, USDA and FDA labeling, laboratory operations, shelf life testing, and environmental regulatory compliance activities.

The impressive résumés of these individuals are only a few of the excellent employees of Ukrop's Homestyle Foods, many of whom were instrumental in propelling the growth of Ukrop's Super Markets that began during the Depression era and grew to become the largest and most popular grocery store chain in the Richmond area. Indeed, people in other parts of the country know about the outstanding reputation of Ukrop's. During vacations in Hilton Head, South Carolina, the Outer Banks of North Carolina, and even Florida, I heard natives in these states inquire about Ukrop's when I mentioned the name of my hometown, Richmond.

In my introduction, I cited the unintended consequences of Adam Smith's invisible hand, in which I said entrepreneurs start their businesses to improve their own lives but end up enriching the lives of their employees, their customers, and their communities. There is no doubt, in my opinion, that the Ukrop family, beginning with the parents of Jim and Bobby, are manifestations of Smith's famous idea. I believe that, if the Ukrop family had not embarked on the path of entrepreneurship, we would have not had the opportunity to share in the success of this organization that has brought its many benefits to so many of us.

Teresa Mason, Health Care Teacher

*Help people help themselves
or save someone's life.*

Some entrepreneurs do not achieve their career objectives until much later in life, which is an accurate description of Teresa Henry Mason, owner and instructor of Hanover county-based Breath of Fresh Air, a health and safety training facility that provides formal classes in many areas of health care for professionals as well as the public.

In fact, some people would have said that finding any type of real success in a business would have been bleak and inauspicious for Mason after she dropped out of high school at sixteen and was clueless about any type of career in the future. However, she did find brief employment as a telephone switchboard operator for the Jefferson Hotel in Richmond in December 1971.

First Job in Health Care

The telephone system was manual in which all incoming calls were routed through a central switchboard before being directed to the recipient of the call. Six months later, she worked for the John Marshall Hotel in the same position as switchboard operator for five cents more an hour. More than one year later, a Revco drugstore in Richmond employed Mason on a part-time basis, which paid another nickel more an hour. However, the position became full time within six months. Meanwhile, she continued to work at the John Marshall Hotel in the evening and on weekends during the first six months of her daytime job at Revco in which she also received benefits.

Teresa Mason in Classroom

Following her three-year employment at Revco in Richmond, she and her former spouse moved to northeast Texas with his family, where she worked in the pharmacy at Titus County Memorial Hospital as an IV (intravenous) admixture technician for three years. Also, while in Texas, she returned to high school at night to earn her general education diploma (GED) in 1978. Thus, it might be said that her job with Revco pharmacy in Richmond and the hospital pharmacy in Texas helped provide the foundation and pave the way for an exciting career in the long-term care pharmacy industry. Furthermore, it enabled her to gain both experience and knowledge in the following years for her own company, Breath of Fresh Air, a CPR and health care training center that she would eventually create.

After leaving Texas in July 1979, she returned to Richmond and worked for Lakeside Pharmacy in which she filled what she termed "twenty-four-hour, forty-eight-hour, and seventy-two-hour unit dose medication cassettes for nursing homes." Four years later, Mason was offered a position as the computer department program manager at

Comp-U-Dose Pharmacy in Richmond. Since there were no computers at this satellite pharmacy at the time, she worked during the first six months in Portsmouth, Virginia, where she learned to operate the system. In fact, Mason said she is amazed at the speed with which technology has advanced in the health care industry.

After having returned to the Richmond pharmacy, she worked with two computer monitors, two three hundred-baud modems, and two telephone handsets that required dialing the pharmacy computer system in Portsmouth. The only time in which she noticed any real speed occurred was when she typed information on one keyboard and then quickly turned and typed on the other keyboard as the data scrolled across the first screen at the pace of a snail.

Throughout her employment at Comp-U-Dose, Mason learned and developed medication dispensing systems, a fact that demonstrates her ability to innovate in technology. She also seized the opportunity to work with multiple computer systems and software programs while converting newly acquired pharmacies in twenty-six states across the United States. Mason remained employed with Com-U-Dose throughout several corporate buyouts and name changes that lasted until September 1996. Today, the pharmacies have been incorporated into the largest long-term care pharmacy in the United States called OmniCare.

A classroom

Her stints in retail pharmacy, combined with the developing techniques in long-term care pharmacy that offered computerized physician orders and medication administration records and multiple medication dispensing systems to assisted living facilities and nursing homes, helped provide the knowledge for her current position as president of Family Care and Cedarfield Pharmacy when it opened in 1996 in the Hermitage at Cedarfield Retirement Community in western Henrico County.

Family Care Pharmacy is also located in Williamsburg and Remington, Virginia, where it offers medications with dispensing systems to long-term care facilities throughout all areas of the state. As one who is obviously good at multitasking, Mason has maintained her responsibilities and title of president at Cedarfield Pharmacy while she has simultaneously owned and operated her own company, Breath of Fresh Air, in Hanover County near Lee-Davis High School. But she admits it has not been an easy task, but one that she shows no signs of abandoning because of her strong desire to help others.

Her business has been a work in progress . In fact,she absorbed everything she could learn from her jobs in pharmacy prior to founding Breath of Fresh Air in 2002. Mason added, "All of this evolved from my mind as I began it, and it has not stopped." In fact, this lady, in similar fashion to KleaneKareTeam's Sharon Dabney-Wooldridge, is motivational and imbued with seemingly boundless energy. It is impossible not to be impressed with her accomplishments, desire, and compassion to help people who are in need. Some might say that her passion to bring health care training certificates to her students is providential.

Teaching Health Care Classes to Anyone

Mason constantly encourages her students to continue their education. She tells them, "Breath of Fresh Air is your stepping stone toward higher education and employment." Most of her classes do not require a GED or high school diploma. She regrets there was not a school similar to Breath of Fresh Air during the years when she was seeking a career without a formal education many years ago. Today, she is determined to offer more opportunities to other persons and finds it somewhat ironic that she had never been without employment since she was sixteen years of age.

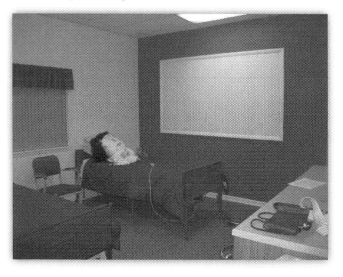

A Class Bedroom

A friend once told Mason that she was a "breath of fresh air," a phrase she adopted as the name of her company and which she literally operated out of her car until she moved into her office in 2007. While she began teaching classes in 1999 in churches and schools, she has taught CPR, first aid training, and other courses in physicians' offices, hospitals, community centers, Ruritan Clubs, country clubs, nursing homes, child care centers, and even outdoors to construction company workers who must be in compliance with OSHA requirements to avoid costly fines and penalties that could boost their insurance premiums.

In the realm of formal education, Mason has obtained her

registered nurse (RN) license and associate's degree in applied health science from Medical Careers Institute, a division of ECPI in Richmond, with a specialty in phlebotomy, the process of drawing blood either for testing or a transfusion. She said her formal education is very important, but her working knowledge of pharmacy and the long-term care industry provided the underpinning to her career and credibility as an instructor.

Currently, Mason and other nurses, who are LPNs and RNs, instruct health care employees as well as the public in the following courses at her office, all of which are now taught in her one-story Mechanicsville, Virginia, building that consists of several classrooms:

- A direct patient care class for assisted living facilities

- Nurse's aide classes

- A medication aide class for assisted living facilities

- A program for medication administration technicians at adult daycares

- Courses for adolescent group homes and correctional facilities

- An annual refresher course of medication aides

- A course for pharmacy technicians

- CPR/AED first aid training for people and their pets

- Babysitter classes

Other classes offered include refresher courses on phlebotomy, dementia, transfer trauma, diabetes, and many other topics needed for continued education. Mason is open to other suggested topics that might benefit people in the community and workplace.

Student in classroom

Mason has taught CPR training to many nurses and other health care providers during the past ten years. However, she is very passionate about teaching the public as well. She said, "I want to help people in general to gain knowledge so they will know there is something they can do to either help themselves or save a life." Importantly, she is willing to be an inspirational speaker for any group or person who seeks to be motivated. Indeed, Teresa Mason, who can multitask as well as anyone with similar talents I have known, is living proof that some people can accomplish many benefits and rewards if they focus on goals and seek to improve the lives of other people.

Stewart Hargrove, Business Insurance Advocate

IAG represents you, the insurance buyer.

The word "insurance" usually conjures up different responses from buyers. As a former commercial property and casualty agent for more than twenty-five years, I am aware of many of these, with some that are cordial and respectful and many others that are not very flattering but downright indignant.

Some people rightly view insurance policies as enigmatic, ambiguous, arcane, and downright confusing, owing to various factors. For example, some buyers of insurance might have had an unfortunate experience resulting from the settlement of a prior claim. Other people truly dislike paying premiums for a policy in which they have never filed a claim resulting from an accident or loss. Compounding the problem is that some agents may fail to explain fully the insurance contract to their clients, a fact that may contribute to the negative and often cynical view that many buyers have of insurance.

Admittedly, the language in a policy might be confusing to buyers and could create the erroneous belief that their own policies should pay for any type of accident. For example, some owners of commercial property insurance policies interpret the "all risk" feature to mean that any hazard or peril is covered, only to learn that it was excluded after an accident. Most agents I have known during my quarter century as a representative of an agency were responsible and concerned about the best interests of their clients. However, some agents fail to inform the buyer of the exclusions on policies that were issued on an "all risks" basis as well as other important facts about the policy.

In addition to the words "all risk," other terms may appear inscrutable and confusing unless explained. Among these are:

- The calculation of the workers' compensation experience modification factor

- NCCI

- BI and PD loss ratios

- A claims made policy

- Monoline policy retention

- A combined single limit policy

Seeking a True Advocate

Because of the reality of the above-listed terms and because it is critically important to insure the clients' assets in an accurate and complete manner, some insurance buyers seek a true advocate who works for them representing their interest alone. In this manner, the insurance advocate is not in the unenviable position of the agent who is under the supervision of a sales manager who pushes incessantly for new sales, a process that prevents the agent from engaging in other activities that are the stock-in-trade of the insurance advocate and benefit the buyer.

In 2000, Stewart Hargrove recognized the need for a true insurance advocate as described above and established his own Hanover County-based company called Insurance Advocacy Group (IAG). Armed with previous experience as an underwriter at an insurance company at its Midwest office and having been a successful property and casualty insurance agent with his father's agency, A.W.

Hargrove Insurance Agency, prior to its sale in 1997, he brings a quarter century of experience in commercial insurance as a genuine and sincere insurance advocate for his clients.

A graduate of Hampton-Sydney College and the recipient of the important and prestigious insurance designation known as chartered property and casualty underwriter (CPCU), Hargrove's company has gained clients in many different industries who seek an advocate who can not only reduce the cost of their insurance premiums by recommending changes in coverage but creating a dialogue with underwriters at insurance companies who are crucial to understanding and protecting the assets of his clients' companies.

Left to right: Dave Murphy, Stewart Hargrove, and John Minor

Four years after creating his company, Hargrove hired John Minor, a highly respected Richmond agent and made him executive vice president. In addition to Minor, who brought a quarter century experience from the agency business, Hargrove employed Dave Murphy, a twenty-eight year veteran who previously worked for

Liberty Mutual Insurance Company. As indicated in a company brochure:

IAG is employed by you as your insurance manager on an outsourced basis. IAG's team of insurance advocates will represent your interests and your interests alone, while navigating your company through the complexities of the insurance industry.

Some of Hargrove's clients tell him that property and casualty insurance is their highest single expense and the one they understand the least.

IAG differs in more than one way from the typical licensed insurance agent who normally reports directly to a sales manager who expects regular reports from the agent that provide details of the number of sales calls made, the expiration date of the prospect's insurance policies, and knowledge of forthcoming sales calls. In many instances, the agent is literally under the thumb of the sales manager and told to focus on new sales and not devote too much time to existing clients. Also differentiating the advocate from the typical agent, IAG does not represent any insurance company. Rather, according to a company brochure, "IAG represents you, the insurance buyer."

Hargrove, an articulate and high-energy guy, elaborated on the important differences of an advocate such as his company from an insurance agent:

> We don't sell insurance nor do we represent any insurance companies ... We use our knowledge of the detail workings of the insurance industry to position our client more effectively to interact with the insurance industry.

Importantly, he cited the reasons for the creation of his company, "We help the agent perform better for his client by having someone who understands the language of the industry, thereby, leveling the communication playing field."

Furthermore, he said:

> Insurance is complicated and expensive, and the buyer is left without a true advocate, such as our company, on staff … For a variety of reasons, your broker or agent may be filtering the information he shares with you and may just not have the time to market your account proactively.

> Consequently, your insurance agent might not have full access to certain markets and a less than satisfactory relationship with the insurance company underwriter he represents.

Working for the Customer

In addition, the client might be buying too much insurance or too little, so Hargrove emphasized that his company provides the client with the missing information so he can have more control over the insurance buying process. He added that, prior to founding his company, there had been no real meaningful change in the manner in which the insurance agent communicated with the underwriter during the previous thirty years as well as the sale of the product by a licensed agent. So he emphasized his company is proactive and treats insurance as a financial product and not solely an underwriting product. Importantly, Hargrove said, "We differ in that we are interested in the factors that influence the financial equation or the cost of money."

Hargrove said the concept of advocacy is broader in its implementation and provides for more than just involvement in the annual insurance renewal process. Due to the complexity of the language in the insurance contract, IAG engages in complicated claims adjustment, audits, and cost analysis. "Advocacy is not just about the purchase of insurance." Importantly, the process of bringing underwriters from insurance companies into the process is critically important since most of them never meet the buyer and do not appear to have an appreciation of the entire process of protecting them from accidents and losses that could affect the assets and employees of their companies. Consequently, the entire relationship with an insurance company, the buyer, and the advocate is a collaborative process. Therefore, he said, "We at IAG bring the underwriters and buyers of insurance together." Because IAG is the buyers' outsourced insurance department, it is very important that they help make their clients and the insurance companies more informed.

In the final analysis, Hargrove said, "It takes an insurance agent, the buyer, an advocate such as IAG, and an underwriter working together as a team for everyone to win."

In the beginning of his career as an insurance advocate, most agents viewed Hargrove with suspicion and dislike. However, after understanding that their clients hired IAG, most agents have become more supportive of his endeavor to reduce the cost of insurance premiums and improve relationships with insurance company underwriters.

Hargrove has suffered a few small setbacks in his business. During the Great Recession of 2008, he said IAG lost five clients. However, he has regained a few of them and added new clients since the housing bust and the near financial implosion of the economy, facts that testify to his growing reputation as a successful advocate for his clients.

In my view, it is important to see the very concept of Stewart Hargrove's IAG venture as an important innovation in an industry that has not demonstrated much change. As a risk taker, Hargrove said:

> I must question the status quo and seek the best value for our own clients and make them aware of the importance of the return on investment (ROI) as a tool for the underwriters to base their premiums.

Arthur Laffer, the founder of the famous Laffer Curve, and Stephen Moore, in their book, *Return to Prosperity*, wrote that some "entrepreneurs bring new disruptive technologies to the market that reorganize the entire concept of product and production."[32] Similarly, David Croslin, former chief technologist at Hewlett-Packard, in an interview with the January 2011 *Entrepreneur* magazine said, "The secret to disruptive innovation is simple: Focus on the customer."[33] In my opinion, both of these statements apply to Stewart Hargrove, whose insurance advocacy company has disrupted the traditional relationship that has existed between agents and companies for a long period of time. Importantly, Hargrove's IAG seeks to bring about constructive change that is beneficial to all parties by placing the customer in charge.

Michael Kelleher, Heating, Air-Conditioning, and Plumbing Entrepreneur

It is all about the customer.

Businesses that sell or provide service in more than one area must differentiate themselves from their competitors. Among those local companies who engage in fuel oil delivery, plumbing, electrical, heating, and air-conditioning, for example, one of them, Kelleher Corporation stands out from the crowd. In fact, according to the current president, Joseph Kelleher, it was the first Richmond-based company to engage simultaneously in all of these areas to increase growth and market share and to be the best of its kind.

Kelleher's ubiquitous orange and blue service trucks create easy customer recognition. Formed in 1968 by the late Michael Kelleher, who had prior experience in delivering home heating oil with another company, this successful family-operated business offers an important lesson that its founder ardently embraced and which many companies sometimes forget. "It is all about the customer," said his articulate and gracious ninety-eight-year-old wife, Marie, chair of the board of a company that still contains his two sons and several grandchildren. Having resigned from a local home heating oil company in the late 1960s, Mike was very determined to create a company that served his customers as if each of them were the only one. With a smile, she said Mike was a very good salesman even if "it took him eight years to ask me to marry him."

Michael Kelleher

His oldest son, Joe, the president of the company and its first driver in 1968, said, "No matter the time of night, Michael Kelleher was there with a genuine concern for his customers to make them comfortable if they had problems with heating or cooling." In fact, Kelleher said a larger company purchased his father's previous employer, a factor that his father believed would de-emphasize the critical importance of customer service.

The Beginning

Michael Kelleher started Kelleher Corporation with one used twenty-eight hundred-gallon oil truck and laid the foundation for a successful diversified company that has boosted sales to over $5 million. In fact, Kelleher said his father built Kelleher Corporation into a multimillion-dollar customer service organization through extraordinary dedication, perseverance, and long hours starting in a twelve-by-twelve room with two desks, three folding beach chairs, and two telephones.

Providing evidence of the difficulty in building his own company, early in the history of the company's history, his father had to forgo his salary for extended periods to assure their vendors were paid on time. But having sacrificed early, Michael Kelleher built Kelleher Corporation into a company that would provide an adequate living for his family and their families.

Marie Kelleher

Starting his new company with heating oil as its main product was not enough if Michael Kelleher desired to grow and offer additional products for his customers. After a short time, the company expanded into the plumbing and electrical businesses. But realizing it needed to fully serve its customers, Kelleher Corporation engaged in not only heating but cooling or air-conditioning in order to provide complete service to local homeowners and small businesses. Importantly,

Kelleher Corporation was the first company in the Richmond area of its kind to install a high-velocity duct system for its customers and to computerize oil operations. Innovation has been important to Kelleher Corporation.

Importance of Customer Service

Many companies stress customer service, but Michael Kelleher believed it passionately. His widow said, "Even if the economy were doing poorly, Mike believed the customer was still the most important part of our business. In fact, they are our employees." Kelleher Corporation solicits the opinions of customers in the immediate aftermath of all service calls. It does not require a Harvard MBA to know that the customer is critical to the success of any business. In fact, all books that discuss the creation of new businesses cite the critical importance of serving the customer, a fact that Kelleher Corporation has done passionately throughout its entire organization and history.

Regarding its own employees, Kelleher Corporation treats them very well since they are the first to see the customer. In fact, Kelleher's employees are trained in its own in-house classes and those sponsored by the Richmond Technical Center. If they pass the required courses, Kelleher Corporation pays the tuition. Importantly, they are paid above-average wages and benefits and can exchange their personal leave time for a Christmas bonus.

The Kelleher Family.

During his nearly four decades at the helm of Kelleher Corporation, Michael Kelleher rejected the urge to diversify into other unknown and unrelated areas, a course of action that several large diversified conglomerates in the late 1960s and 1970s practiced much to the regret of many of them. In fact, according to Joe Kelleher, his father decided against:

- Selling coin-operated ice machines

- Purchasing a battery-operated appliance truck that moved heavy objects up and down stairways

- Selling and providing service on SpacePak high-velocity residential cooling and heating systems

- Selling automatic lawn irrigation systems

- Selling ear, nose, and throat medical instruments

- Featuring a product called Vapor Mid, a transparent, plastic, water-filled pyramid that, when connected to an oil burner, causes it to operate at over 80 percent efficiency without losing any of its water

Kelleher said his father was aware of the challenges his company confronted. For example, Michael Kelleher understood many competitors were in Richmond. Moreover, he was fifty-seven years old in 1968 with very little start-up capital when he started his company. Despite the odds against success, Joe Kelleher said, "The driving force that motivates Mike Kelleher is his untiring desire to serve his customers."

Like many other businesses that comprise a part of the US economy, heating and air-conditioning companies are commonly grouped in the HVAC industry, which refers to heating, ventilating, and air-conditioning. According to information from Wikipedia, this industry has benefited from inventions and discoveries made by individuals such as Willis Carrier, Nicolay Lvov, Michael Faraday, Reuben Trane, James Joule, William Rankine, Sadi Camot, and others.[34]

Kelleher employees

Based on information supplied by the online industry service, IBIS World, there were 88,443 companies in the HVAC industry in 2010. These HVAC companies employed 87,560 individuals who provided heating and cooling services to homeowners and companies in the United States.[35]

The technology in the HVAC industry benefits from upgrades and improvements at various periods of time, some of which the government mandates. According to Fluid Solution's online service, President George W. Bush signed the Energy Policy Act in 2005, which provided incentives for traditional energy production as well as newer, more efficient technologies and conservation. "Most notably," the reports said, "the act sets minimum efficiency standards for sixteen consumer and commercial products, including commercial unit heaters and large commercial air conditioners." Moreover, the report claimed, "HVAC accounts for 40 to 60 percent of the energy used in US commercial and residential buildings. This represents an opportunity for energy savings using proven technologies and design concepts."[36]

Kelleher Service Truck

During its more than four decades of history, Kelleher Corporation has won the following awards:

- The Richmond Chamber of Commerce Small Business of the Year Award (1981)

- The Retail Merchants Association of Greater Richmond Retailer of the Year (1993)

- The Better Business Bureau of Central Virginia's Torch Award for Workplace Ethics (2004)

- The US Small Business Administration's Regional Small Business of the Year Award (2008)

Perhaps contributing to the above awards, Kelleher Corporation was the first local company to hire an African American employee, George Noel, who became vice president. Contributing to its excellent service and technical ability, Kelleher said his company requires the presence of three officers in the field at all times to assist technicians, if required.

Founder Michael Kelleher's unstinting commitment to service is strongly embraced by not only the employees of his company today but by its current owners who believe it as passionately as Michael Kelleher did during his years at the helm. In fact, his wife Marie, a charming and self-deprecating lady, constantly echoes her late husband. A highly regarded swimmer, who has won medals in senior Golden Olympics competition and still swims regularly at a local YMCA pool, she works most days of the week and intends to carry on her husband's commitment to customer service in the same fashion as her children and grandchildren.

Wayne Hazzard, Electrical and General Contractor

Aptitude is important, but attitude is everything.

I gained my first glimpse of Wayne Hazzard's discipline and ability to focus during a card game at an overnight and out-of-town golf outing in the early 1980s. During one evening, each player at the card table was consuming some type of alcohol except Hazzard. I never asked him the reason for his abstinence on that evening, but I have grown to believe that too much alcohol would affect his ability to concentrate on the important facts at the moment. Also, I feel certain it would have impaired his ability to become successful and reach new heights as an entrepreneur.

Being focused at the right moment has been important to Hazzard over the years. His parents demanded good behavior from both he, a former Boy Scout, and his two brothers, but they allowed their boys the freedom in which to pursue their dreams.

Like many students in high school, Hazzard did not know the career path he would choose later in life. However, during his junior year in high school, a teacher encouraged him to enroll in the industrial co-op program, a program that led to his first job at Virginia Machine Works. He said jokingly, "I made $1.35 an hour, and, at times, the job was so slow that we greased bridges." But his parents told him, "Aptitude is important, but attitude is everything." It's advice he never forgot.

Following his first job at Virginia Machine Works, Hazzard worked for both H.P. Foley Electrical and Ben Collier Electrical at separate periods of time and for a few years under their apprentice programs. Hazzard never had been a supporter of labor unions. As a Boy Scout, he said he was taught that God, family, and country were the most important values. However, he said unions viewed their organizations equally as important as the Boy Scout values, a belief he did not share.

Wayne Hazzard

Formation of Company

After working for Collier Electrical, Hazzard decided to form his own electrical contracting company, a venture that began on January 1, 1975, and which he operated from his home. He also built a beauty salon for his wife, Nancy, which she operated for one year in their house following the creation of his company, Hazzard Electrical Corporation. Within a few months of operations, Hazzard had obtained several large contracts from companies, which enabled him to move into a building located in a Hanover County park north of Richmond and hire employees.

Starting a business is never an easy venture, particularly in the 1970s when OPEC had increased petroleum prices to record levels, causing inflation to jump and joblessness to increase to over 8 percent during most of the decade. In fact, interest rates soared to the high teens, making the cost of capital prohibitive for many smaller businesses.

In hindsight, Hazzard's decision to become an entrepreneur was a good one despite the less than favorable conditions during the formation of his company. He said that starting a new venture during a recession or a weak economy is better than beginning one at or near the top of the business cycle, a remark that is indicative of a wise investor. A compelling reason for beginning a new business during an economic slowdown is that some competitors might have closed operations, merged with other similar companies, or chosen to enter a different trade.

Hazzard learned quickly that he could not manage his business, install electrical wiring, provide prompt service to his customers, and pursue growth simultaneously unless he desired to remain a very small company. In fact, he said he had no idea what he was doing at first. But realizing he already knew the process of installing electrical wiring, he understood that, in order to achieve growth in his new company, he had to hire more capable electricians because he really needed to learn how to run and manage a business.

The electrical contracting industry, according to Hoovers, an online industry research site, includes about seventy thousand firms like Hazzard Electrical with total combined revenues of $11 billion. Major national companies include EMCOR Group, Rosendin Electric, Integrated Electric Services, MYR Group, and Bergelectric Corp. Like other industries discussed in this book, the electrical contracting industry is highly fragmented, containing more of the so-called mom-and-pop variety. Most small firms generate less than $2 million in sales and employ about ten people.[37]

Finding a Niche

To obtain new customers, Hazzard engaged in soliciting new customers and found a niche in the grocery store industry, an industry that included Safeway, Colonial, and other similar national chains as his customers. Hazzard's electrical contracting company grew rapidly, and he learned by experiencing the hard knocks of being a business owner. He always told his employees that the key to their success was customer service because they never wanted a customer to say that their service was bad. Moreover, he admitted that times were hard in the beginning and it was difficult to make payroll.

In addition to engaging in the wiring of national chain store buildings in Richmond, Hazzard Electrical rewired an entire fourteen-story building in Greenville, South Carolina, and a Veterans Affairs building in Salem, Virginia. In addition, the company installed new electrical wiring for Marlowe Furniture's showroom building in Alexandria, Virginia, and a new Sydnor and Hundley furniture store located in Chesterfield County across the James River from the city of Richmond.

Hazzard Electrical headquarters in 1975

Importantly, his company's growth had reached the point at which he knew that providing excellent customer service was as important as good employee relations. Regarding the latter, he paid bonuses to his employees and began a very popular annual Christmas party for both employees and customers that still bring back many fond memories to those who attended them. He also hired many competent people, such as Ken Hubbard, who became his treasurer, and Earl Crowder, Jimmy Robertson, and Larry Leadbetter, all of whom would prove to be important to his future plans in the construction industry as they were to the early history of Hazzard Electrical.

Like many successful entrepreneurs, innovation was important to Hazzard. In the early 1980s, as the election of Ronald Reagan as president appeared to have removed the dark cloud that hung over the economy during the 1970s, Hazzard's company invented a device that allowed gasoline stations to reset the pump from the inside of the store. The product boosted the growth of his company and confidence of its employees.

Hazzard also created a separate subsidiary known as Hazzard

Service Company that provided routine repairs to the customers of Hazzard Electrical. Ken Hubbard headed that division. In 1984, Hazzard, who desired to explore a new general contracting venture, sold Hazzard Electrical to a few of his employees, with Hubbard becoming president of the service entity and Earl Crowder becoming president of the original electrical company that Hazzard founded. Within a few years of the spin-off, Hazzard Service became known as Express Electric with Hubbard as its president.

Creating His Second Company

Thus, Hazzard embarked on a new venture and sold his first company that had provided a start to his career in construction. The highest number of employees at Hazzard Electrical reached fifty-five during his period of ownership. Moreover, the sale of his first company provided an opportunity for Ken Hubbard, the new owner, to hire workers and achieve growth as an entrepreneur.

One of Hazzard's reasons for exiting the electrical contracting industry was that subcontractors, such as Hazzard Electrical, were often slow to get paid by general contractors and other organizations that headed the construction job. So he wanted to gain a position of more control and strength through the sale of his electrical contracting company and the formation of a new construction company that could exert more control over the entire process. Also, he desired a new challenge that he and his new partner, Larry Dorset, found when they built their new Hanover County-based company, Professional Contractors, into a large commercial general contracting firm that erected new buildings and provided repairs and renovations for their new customers. Known as Pro-Con, Hazzard's new company not only used new employees, it hired subcontractors to perform some of the labor, thereby providing them with a source of income. While the number of employees can fluctuate within one company, Pro-Con's subcontractors, which, when combined with his own employees at the general contracting company, could total between thirty and forty.

Pro-Con Building

Among some of the projects completed by Pro-Con were:

- A new building at the US Army training base at Fort Lee, Virginia, located twenty-five miles southeast of Richmond

- A large Safeway store

- A fourteen thousand-square-foot structure warehouse building for Coca-Cola Bottling Company located in Elizabeth City, North Carolina

In early 2001, Hazzard still owned and operated Pro-Con, but Dorset left the company in 1995 to engage in a new venture, thereby paving the way for Hazzard's longtime close friend and business colleague, Larry Leadbetter, to become the driving force behind the company. Calling Leadbetter "one of the best and most important people that I hired in my life at Hazzard Electrical," Hazzard called him indispensable. In fact, Hazzard emphasized his positive view of Leadbetter when he said:

> He (Larry Leadbetter) is one of the best things that has happened to me in my life. He has been with me through good times and bad ones, and, even the years we were apart when he owned half of Express Electric, we remained very close.

Furthermore, Hazzard said Leadbetter's attitude and willingness to work are only surpassed by his loyalty. Hazzard is convinced that, without Leadbetter, his journey would have been much more difficult.

One could be forgiven for believing that Hazzard would be content with having created two successful companies. But they would overlook the energy and talent that lay within the man. Several years ago, a friend asked him for a loan. Instead of readily giving him money, Hazzard talked the friend into allowing him to become a co-owner of Virginia Specialty Products, a Hanover county-based company that sells and installs commercial and industrial roll-up doors, dock equipment, and miscellaneous related items. It has employed as many as fifteen persons in the past and continues to engage in its field of trade.

Serving His County

In addition to Hazzard's successful entrepreneurial ventures, he cares deeply about his native Hanover County, a county in which he hopes to represent the South Anna District as a representative to the Board of Supervisors in late 2011. Hazzard has been chairman of the South Anna Republican Committee for the past year of 2010.

A fiscal and social conservative, who supports strong economic growth in the private sector, Hazzard is philosophically closer to the Tea Party movement that embraces spending restraints in all areas of government. Drawing a comparison to Hanover County's increase in population of 15.7 percent from 2000 to 2010, Hazzard said its budget increased 107 percent. Consequently, he believes there needs to be a greater scrutiny in the growth of our government because we can make budget cuts without reducing further services to our citizens.

Assuming that Hazzard is elected, I doubt he would cease using his formidable talents and knowledge as an entrepreneur and contractor in some fashion. Moreover, I expect him to encourage other younger people to become entrepreneurs as he has done and boost economic growth in the United States. His decision to start a new business venture in the depths of an economic recession, combined with his innovative talents, his ability to delegate authority to competent employees, his belief in close employee relations, and satisfied customers, all of these help define the entrepreneurial talents of Wayne Hazzard.

Michael Kasmir and Dan Wolford, Staffing Company Founders

We were poor, hungry and determined.

In the nineteenth century, the famous American writer, Horatio Alger, wrote stories about young men who worked their way from the bottom to the top of the economic ladder, an example that is applied to other entrepreneurs in this book. Michael Kasmir and Dan Wolford, both of whom became close friends at the University of Maryland, embody the classic Horatio Alger success story.

Both of these high-energy guys began their own company, Kaztronix, in 2003 in the basement of Wolford's mother's house and have grown their enterprise into a highly respected Northern Virginia-based staffing company that seeks to supply personnel for the government and telecommunication, cable television, technology, health care, and scientific industries. Kasmir said, "Both of us began at the bottom and always had a passion to start our own business." Wolford established his first monetary goal of independence when he was eight years of age, and he has attained it.

Kasmir, who heads the telecom and technology division of Kaztronix from the Dulles Airport region in northern Virginia, gained an early knowledge of the staffing industry as an intern at Spherion. Wolford established Kaztronix's New Jersey office following the formation of the company where he performs staffing for biotechnology and large pharmaceutical companies in the Mid-Atlantic, Northeast, and West Coast.

Specific Types of Employees

Both Wolford and Kasmir recruit employees with high levels of skills that relate to their specialty. Thus, Wolford seeks employees who are knowledgeable in clinical trials, research and development, and production, areas that are critically important to pharmaceutical and biotechnology companies. Also included in the health care industry are professionals trained in nursing and pharmacy operations. Similarly, Kasmir recruits candidates whose technical skills relate to the information technology and telecommunication industries.

In the nearly eight years since the creation of Kaztronix, the company has grown its sales to $20 million and employs more than two hundred and fifty people. Importantly, it has received fifty-ninth place among the Inc. 500 companies in the human resources segment. Its customers recognize Kaztronix as a very customer-oriented enterprise, and Kasmir seeks to penetrate the middle market where there are more employees and the opportunity in networking and cyber security is huge.

Companies do not grow and become successful by accident. Kasmir reported that Kaztronix has become successful for several important reasons, including its decision to be a leader in specific industries. As evidence of this desire for specialization, Kaztronix overcame challenges in the beginning by becoming niche-oriented in telecom and other industries, enabling them to overcome some of the competition. Prior to entering an industry or soliciting business from a company, Kaztronix:

- Researches new technologies

- Conducts an assessment of the company and the industry in which it operates

- Seeks to understand the core competencies of the company

This is so Kaztronix can demonstrate to their customers that they understand their business and they can help them to continue to grow their companies. Kasmir said, "We tell our employees that success results from following up with the customers and demonstrating you are determined to help them to grow their own businesses."

"We Were Poor, Hungry, and Determined"

Kasmir also said it is critically important that Kaztronix hire the most qualified people for its clients. Perhaps thinking about the background of both he and Wolford, Kasmir seeks employees who are self-motivated. Importantly, he added, "Like Dan and I, they should be PHD, which I define as poor, hungry, and determined."

Kasmir said it is important to understand that they (he and Wolford) were poor, hungry, and determined, but learned to work hard and demonstrated they knew how to be persistent in solving the needs of their clients. This helped to generate referrals for them, which are important to the company's own future growth. Both of these entrepreneurs are as energetic today as they were when they created their company. In fact, they are always looking over their shoulders to maintain a lead over their competition, a fact that keeps them focused and always thinking about how to provide the best service to their clients.

Dan Wolford and Michael Kasmir

Price is not always the main factor in obtaining new clients. Rather, Kasmir added it is "the quality of service that we have performed for our existing client base that may determine if we acquire a new account." Importantly, both Wolford and Kasmir agree that diversification has been important to the growth of Kaztronix. Wolford stressed the importance of being engaged in more than one area of concentration. Representing more than one industry helped Kaztronix navigate the worst of the economic recession of 2008. In addition, hard work, motivation, and relationships have benefited his company.

During an evening interview with Kasmir at his home in Arlington, he took a phone call from an employee at 7:45 p.m., who discussed a promising sales call on the same day.

"That guy is PHD," he said with a smile after the call. "Like Dan and me."

Kasmir continued, "We want our employees to be not only self-motivated and to work hard, but we hope they will be financially successful as well." In fact, Kasmir said there is nothing wrong with wanting to be very successful in addition to other important values in life. "Being motivated to make more money will be good not only for Kaztroniz, it will also benefit the employees because we care deeply about the people who work for Kaztronix and their families." He also said that his company provided contributions to several charity organizations in its geographical areas.

More Growth Potential

The life sciences, biotechnology, and pharmaceutical areas of Kaztronix present exciting areas of growth potential. Initially, the attempt to grow this specialty did not work out in the Washington metro area along the Highway 270 area in Maryland. Therefore, to grab some of this business, Dan was located in northern New Jersey, where he focuses on companies in the Mid-Atlantic, New England, and West Coast areas of the United States.

Kaztronix Staff

Kasmir said there is a huge need and great opportunity for this specialty in pharmaceuticals and biotech. To gain experience in the business world, Wolford sold Microsoft Windows computer systems in college to pay his tuition and other living expenses. He was not born rich. Importantly, Kasmir said his partner was a top performer at GSX, a company where he placed Wolford during his early employment at his first job in the staffing industry.

"He understands what it means to start at the bottom," Kasmir added.

In addition to telecom, biotech, and pharmaceutical staffing, Kaztronix provides services for the technology industry at large. These include operative support, development, data management, and infrastructure service. Kaztronix's commitment to providing very competent employees is as important to technology companies as it is to its other areas of specialty. Also, working in Kaztronix's favor is Kasmir's previous reference to becoming niche-oriented in its specialty markets, which, according to Mansel Blackford's history on small business, has been a decisive factor in enabling smaller companies such as his and others to survive in a competitive economy.[38]

According to a March 6, 2011 online report from the America Staffing Association (ASA):

> The US staffing industry is anticipated to grow faster and add more jobs over the next decade than any other industry ... By helping businesses tap the talent they need when they need it, America's staffing companies improve the efficiency of the US labor force. By quickly matching talent to work, America's staffing companies boost US employment. By creating jobs, America's staffing companies strengthen the US economy.[39]

Kaztronix provides liberal benefits, for example, health insurance that includes dental, vision, and prescription drug coverage as well as life and disability coverage and a 401(k) retirement plan, for its diverse group of employees on the first day of employment.

Kasmir said:

> They are very important to us ... We desire employees who maximize the potential for the company by boosting our overall productivity, creating a sense of cohesiveness and loyalty to our client base.

Kaztronix has also adopted a new method in which to store employee résumés and make them more readily available to their clients, a process that should be highly beneficial to them by enhancing efficiencies. Kaztronix is keenly focused on providing the best employees to its clients who strive to boost the productivity of their operations in a more competitive economy.

Suzanne Wolstenholme, Catering Company Owner

Voted best caterer.

As a young girl, one of Suzanne Wolstenholme's dreams was to own and operate a bed-and-breakfast inn in her native historic Hanover County. Her dream was not realized precisely as she had hoped. However, little did she know at the time that her future company, Homemades by Suzanne, would become the most well-known and respected caterer in the Richmond metro area.

Prior to going into business as a caterer, Suzanne prepared meals at a local Hanover County church with friends and family, who provided her with the confidence to become an entrepreneur and helped pave the way for her to own and operate a catering company in 1982. Moreover, Suzanne's parents encouraged her to enter the catering business, which, according to First Research, an online service that profiles different industries, consists of about eight thousand caterers in the United States.[40]

Like some other industries, catering is fragmented, with the top fifty companies representing less than 15 percent of total industry revenue. According to First Research, the estimated total revenue in the industry is about $8 billion, which results from many different types of catering events, including weddings, birthday celebrations, business and religious meetings, and other gatherings.[41]

Combined with her catering venture, Suzanne opened a popular restaurant named Homemades by Suzanne in Ashland in 1982 near the railroad tracks and within walking distance of the highly regarded liberal arts college, Randolph Macon. Not only does she serve lunches to college students and the local townspeople, Suzanne also prepares box lunches, deli buffet trays, gift baskets, and homemade breads and bakery items for both lunchtime patrons and dinner, too. She also provides delivery service to homes and local businesses.

Suzanne's Ashland Restaurant

Suzanne provides catering for corporate events, weddings, and other festive occasions, including social gatherings for Virginia's state legislative body, the general assembly. Her banquet facility is located at the elegant Colony Club, which is housed in an early twentieth-century building on West Franklin Street next to the historic Kent-Valentine House (built in 1845) and Linden Row Hotel in downtown Richmond, Virginia.

Catering Weddings

Many business meetings and social events, including weddings and rehearsal receptions, are held at the Colony Club, and Suzanne caters all of them. In fact, in early 2011, she estimated she has provided catering services to more than eleven hundred weddings since the creation of her business. In late 2011, Suzanne is planning to open a new and larger banquet and wedding reception facility at the newly renovated historic John Marshall Hotel (built in 1920) in the Virginia Room and located a few blocks east of the Colony Club.

Colony Club Location

According to the US Census Bureau's report that was released in January 2011, population has increased in the city of Richmond, a fact that appears to justify Suzanne's plans to expand further into the capital city as the apparent renaissance of the historic downturn area continues to manifest itself.

A catering business might not require the type of innovations that many industries embrace to maintain growth or at least keep up with change. However, her decisions to locate at both the historic Colony Club and John Marshall Hotel in downtown Richmond are innovative because they are new locations and away from her roots in Hanover County. Moreover, they indicate her desire to be part of the changing dynamics of growth in the city of Richmond.

Perhaps unknown to many people, Suzanne indicated that most caterers do not enjoy wedding events. A few years ago, she was surprised to learn during her attendance at a caterers convention in Las Vegas that most of the attendees preferred non-wedding events. This was good news to Suzanne's ears because her company thrives on and enjoys catering weddings. Moreover, her employees share her enthusiasm since she can use as many as fifty of them to host a wedding or even other large social events. In most cases, her employee count averages in the low twenties. Some of her employees have been with her since the inception of her business.

Proposed John Marshall location

Suzanne's husband, Warren, performs the logistics of catering for his wife and the financial aspects of her company. With the exception of a few online ads, there is almost no traditional newspaper and radio advertising. Instead, word of mouth and online advertising are the preferred methods to cater more events. In an online ad entitled "A Special Place for Special Events," the website ad extols the elegance of the Colony Club with the following words:

> The interior of the Colony Club is traditional Richmond with antique sideboards, convertible sofas, and wing chairs, accented with Oriental rugs. We offer a lovely bride's room with a full-length mirror and dressing table. A perfect setting for candid photographs.

The lack of traditional print advertising has not hurt Suzanne's reputation. In fact, *Richmond* magazine has voted Homemades by Suzanne "best caterer" for four consecutive years. Her customers come regardless of the fact that they do not engage in advertising. Her loyal staff prepares all food with the exception of delicious cheesecakes that are imported from New York.

Suzanne outside Colony Club.

In addition to the previous description of the Colony Club, it also features a ballroom with a parquet dance floor with the ability to contain two hundred and fifty guests for a cocktail buffet reception and up to one hundred and twenty patrons for a seated dinner as well as a brick outdoor courtyard under the trees that is ideal for outside activities such as small wedding ceremonies in the daytime or at night.

An Excellent Reputation

Building an excellent reputation over a quarter century required lots and lots of sacrifices. Unlike many other Americans, Suzanne and her husband are unable to take many vacations in the summer months and other popular holidays, owing to the fact that many social functions occur during these periods of time. She does not complain about the lack of more personal time since she enjoys what she is doing.

Former Republican Vice President Nominee Sarah Palin provided some drama for Suzanne during the 2008 presidential campaign when she visited the Ashland restaurant. Ms. Palin specifically desired to talk to a women's group during the trip to the Richmond area, and she made sure her security guards were present during her visit to the Ashland restaurant near the railroad tracks.

Suzanne represents or embodies many of the qualities that people expect from a caterer. She is gracious, exudes serenity, and demonstrates professionalism at all times. In fact, she is the type of person who many people want to be their caterer. Families paying for weddings have complete confidence in her ability to cater the marital celebration after the vows are taken because catering weddings are her largest source of revenue. Importantly, she has created jobs, produced a superior product or service that benefits the community, and improved the life for her own family.

Michael O'Neil, Health Care Entrepreneur

I felt a complete lack of empowerment.

It may be safe to say that most people who have been discharged from a hospital don't give serious thought to improving the experiences of other patients at the institution even if it was not entirely a good one for them. Not so for Michael O'Neil. At twenty-eight years of age in 1999 and engaged to his fiancée, Wendy, he was in his final year of graduate school at Georgetown University when a diagnosis of non-Hodgkin's lymphoma, a blood cancer, caused him to contemplate methods to improve patient care at hospitals that he would later seek to implement as an entrepreneur.

Labeling his clinical care at Johns Hopkins Hospital in Baltimore as terrific, O'Neil, who received his undergraduate degree in political science from Notre Dame before completing his MBA at Georgetown, said the patient experience was not so good. "I felt like I was on the outside looking in on my own care without access to the depth of information and understanding of the procedures, medications, and treatment options. I felt out of control."

Elaborating further on his experience in the hospital, he said it wasn't that anyone was treating him poorly. Rather, his words provided the philosophical underpinning to his idea to improve health care as an entrepreneur, "It was so evident that the entire system does not place the patient in the center of the process."

Describing his stay in a hospital in very moving comments on his website, he said:

> I remember it like it was yesterday ... I spent countless hours staring aimlessly at an outdated TV. The days grew longer. I craved information about my condition, communication with friends and family, and connectivity to the outside world.

Most important to him, he felt a complete loss of empowerment. He knew there had to be a better way.

Improving Hospital Experience

O'Neil's less than satisfactory overall experience at the hospital provided the impetus for him to establish his own company in 1999, GetWellNetwork, a Bethesda, Maryland-based company that is the leader in interactive patient care solutions. Having invented the concept known as Interactive Patient Care (IPC), GetWellNetwork's program empowers the patient in many aspects of hospital care and ultimately seeks to realize better efficiencies and lower costs in overall health care spending. In fact, it has received the exclusive endorsement of the prestigious American Hospital Association. A patent is pending on the product.

Patient Pathways is GetWellNetwork's interactive process of guiding the patient through a unique path of tasks and education. By using their hospital room TV monitors, patients are empowered because they learn more about their care, medical condition and safety, and such processes as patient discharge, medication teaching during and after their hospital stay, and various aspects of patient education. This patient-centered approach improves efficiencies in overall health care and enhances the quality of health care by placing patients in the driver seat for their care.

GetWellNetwork embraces what O'Neil calls "5 Commitments," which form the foundation and reason for his company's existence.

These commitments do not change, but they guide the company's employees daily. Despite changes in company strategy, operations, and outside macroeconomic events, O'Neil and the company are unwavering in their commitments.

1. To our <u>patients</u>: To improve their health care experience

2. To our <u>nurses and doctors</u>: To provide them with an essential patient care tool

3. To our <u>customers (hospitals)</u>: To deliver measurable outcomes and return on investments

4. To our <u>employees</u>: To develop them to their fullest potential

5. To our <u>shareholders</u>: To deliver shareholder value and return

In addition to his company's 5 Commitments, O'Neil has embraced what he calls his own individual commitment, as quoted below under "My Leadership Constitution" and invites "all our employees to challenge if I ever I am not living up to it."

My Leadership Constitution

I DECLARE THAT I AM passionate, creative, positive, and influential. I am a change agent and a leader. I am open and honest. I value integrity and family above everything. I am competitive and ambitious, and I am energized by people coming together to win. I am a survivor. Lastly, I am humbled and grateful for life's blessing each day, yet bold in my ability and responsibility to make the world better. YOU CAN COUNT ON ME TO bring bold, new ideas that move people and industries forward even in the face of great challenges and resistance. I will always tell the truth, even when the message is difficult to deliver or to hear. You can count on me to be a team player, as well as an effective coach, and include others in key decisions. I will make the tough call when necessary and bring endless energy, creativity, and focus when the stakes are the highest.

Gaining New Hospital Clients

Since the advent of GetWellNetwork's IPC program, one hundred hospitals with fifteen thousand beds have adopted it. There are currently some five thousand hospitals in the United States with over 1 million beds, facts that indicate there is plenty of room for O'Neil's company, which has one hundred and twenty-five employees, to continue its growth.

The effectiveness of GetWellNetwork's program is detailed in a brochure on the concept of patient engagement in hospitals, which, according to O'Neil, "is a core strategy to improve performance of health care providers and patient outcomes." For example, in the area of medication teaching, which is designed to achieve patient satisfaction, nurses attempt to make patients aware of the purpose of the medication and possible side effects. Christiana Care Health Care System of Delaware embraced this strategy, prompting the hospital to generate improvements of 14 percent in patient satisfaction. Similarly, in the realm of staff responsiveness or, in what the brochure terms, "Help as soon as wanted," three Flagler hospitals in Florida demonstrated noticeable improvements of an average of 18 percent over previous data. Importantly, in the area of operations improvement, which includes reduction in average length of stay, the Seton Medical Center in Williamson, Texas, demonstrated an 8 percent reduction, resulting in a cost savings of $112,420.

One of GetWellNetwork's main selling features in the section of ROI/operations improvement is that patient engagement can improve "Nursing Workflow Efficiency," a concept that the brochure said is manifest at Virginia's Winchester Medical Center, which experienced a reduction in six hundred and thirty-seven nursing hours over a three-month period "with automated pain assessment documentation." Importantly, this improvement resulted in an annual estimated cost saving of $165,218 to the medical center. Similarly, in the area of operations improvement, the Florida Hospital Altamonte in Altamonte Springs, Florida, reported a reduction in 1,172 non-clinical tasks off-loaded from regular nurses in the first five months. This significant improvement resulted in a 50 percent reduction in call button requests to the nursing station.

Michael O'Neil and Family

Also, in the important area of revenue growth, cross referrals-retail pharmacy, the Medical University in Charleston, South Carolina, reported an increase of $214,327 in pharmacy revenue in a six- month period. Patients who fill their prescriptions at the hospital pharmacy just prior to checkout help boost hospital revenues. In addition to added benefits from patient prescriptions, mammography benefited the Valley Medical Center in the state of Washington by boosting cancer screening services and the West Jefferson Medical Center in Marrero, Louisiana, which experienced an 11 percent increase in revenue through mammogram referrals. In other measurable areas of patient engagement—pain control, environment of care, care measures (CM), quality, and safety—hospitals reported significant improvements that led to either a reduction in costs and/or an increase in revenue. All of this good news is music to the ears of hospital management teams who are clients of O'Neil's company, and it should be of profound interest to health care providers who are not customers of GetWellNetwork.

Improving Patient Access

GetWellNetwork enables hospital patients to utilize Patient Pathways from their hospital beds, a process that transforms their in-room television sets into a complete interactive experience that benefits not only the patient but health care providers as well. From their own beds, for example, patients can use a wireless keyboard or electronic device such as a touch screen or handheld products and access hospital information, educational literature, entertainment choices, and many other forms of information relating to medical patient data. Very importantly, all information transmitted by patients from the keyboards in their hospital room is simultaneously sent to what O'Neil called "a Web-based reporting tool and dashboards to nurses, doctors, and hospital leaders so they can keep a real-time pulse of how their patients are feeling about the care they are receiving." This is a huge benefit for both the patient and health care providers since both parties are not kept in the dark. Moreover, the lines of communication are much closer and open, a process that should enable the nursing staff and hospital administrators to achieve more efficient operations and perhaps boost their own profits.

Other benefits from Patient Pathways include education on the patient's medical condition, including special programs called heart failure care plan, pain management, fall prevention, hand hygiene, deep vein thrombosis, the pediatric asthma care plan, smoking cessation tests, and procedures, that can be obtained according to a company brochure from the GetWellNetwork patient library. In addition, Patient Pathways provides access to e-mail, instant messages, and what a GetWellNetwork brochure labels as "a full Internet browsing experience that includes plug-ins for Web technologies like Flash and streaming video."

Reducing Hospital Costs

O'Neil said that nursing care costs represents the largest single expense to hospitals, a factor that his company's Blueprint for Success methodology as well as the Patient Engagement process may help reduce. For example, according to one of his brochures:

> The Blueprint for Success aligns the GetWellNetwork solution with the outcomes most important to the hospital (by engaging) hospital leadership, integrating GetWellNetwork into the care process, empowering clinicians and staff to take action, and ensuring the delivery of world-class service to patients and their caregivers.

Thus, patients who take the initiative to learn more about their own medical condition and other routine, non-emergency information from GetWellNetwork can eliminate unnecessary burdens from the nursing staff, thereby enabling them to focus more of their considerable skills on patients with serious, life-threatening conditions.

An ill-informed person who embraces erroneous facts about health care prior to entering a hospital may not be the best patient. However, if the patient chooses a hospital that subscribes to GetWellNetwork's IPC process, the person is likely to be better informed and a more satisfied patient after being discharged. Similarly, the hospital that adopts GetWellNetwork's IPC is likely to offer more efficient and patient-friendly care. Very importantly, the hospital will be more productive and could realize higher profits.

It appears that GetWellNetwork's IPC could be an important factor in assisting hospitals during the transition to health care reform (what many call ObamaCare) or, more precisely, the Patient Protection and Affordable Care Act that Congress passed in 2010. For example, those hospitals that purchase GetWellNetwork's IPC program may offset unforeseen costs or less revenue from ObamaCare if they adopt

Michael O'Neil's company's program. In fact, O'Neil says the new health care law forces health care providers to give proper care, or it hits their reimbursements.

Like most entrepreneurs, Michael O'Neil has made mistakes. "We fail sometimes, but it is not daunting." In fact, he has lost accounts and made mistakes, but, importantly, he emphasized he has not wavered from his commitments to the patients, the hospitals and health care providers, his employees, and shareholders.

I first met Michael O'Neil on a flight from Baltimore to San Antonio in March 2011. During the approximate three and half hour journey, I noticed the intensity and focus with which he operated the keyboard on his laptop. I could tell he was fully engaged in his business, a fact that should reassure all parties named in his "5 Commitments." We exchanged some brief comments during the flight, and I asked for his business card because I intuitively believed he might be a good candidate for this book. Innovative companies such as Michael O'Neil's GetWellNetwork are paving the way toward true health care reform, which should benefit all parties in this critically important area.

In my opinion, entrepreneurs such as Michael O'Neil also help vindicate Art Laffer and Steve Moore's view in their book, *Return to Prosperity*, where they wrote:

> Consumers and workers benefit above and beyond where they otherwise would have been. These entrepreneurs bring new "disruptive" technologies to the market that reorganizes the entire concept of product and production.[42]

David Watson, Machinist and Engineer

Practicing the Golden Rule every day.

Like Bobby Ukrop who returned to work as an entrepreneur after the sale of his company, David Watson never learned to retire for a very long period of time. At age sixty-five and after forty years working in process control instrumentation, desiccant dehumidifier design, and production and machine tool sales, Watson created his own fabrication company, Watson Machine Corporation, now located in Powhatan County in 1992.

Born in 1926 and six years before the Great Depression, Watson was one of eleven children with six brothers and four sisters. His father died when he was six years old, so his mother, Epsie, who failed to complete high school, reared him. It was very fitting that former Virginia Governor Miles Godwin chose her as Mother of the Year in 1967. Watson said it was special for him to visit Governor Godwin's office with his mother to receive the award. He described her as his rock. He said, "No matter what took place, I knew she loved me."

Prior to college, Watson enlisted as an air corps cadet. All of his brothers served in the armed forces during and after World War II. During his basic training, the war ended, but he served on the island of Guam and the Philippines. He was assigned to the Air Corps Headquarters Squadron in Tokyo, which was located two blocks from General Douglas MacArthur's headquarters and across the moat from the Japanese emperor's palace.

Shortly after graduation from Hampden Sydney in 1951, where he received a bachelor of science degree in science and physics, Watson met his future wife, Marie House, during a time when he was filling in for a teacher at Wilson Memorial High School in Fishersville, Virginia. She was the physical education teacher at the high school and the tenth child of a German dairy farmer, John House.

First Job in a Plant

Watson decided not to pursue teaching, owing to an unattractive salary of $2,100 a year. Instead, after learning that DuPont Construction was hiring for its Savannah River Plant on 114,000 acres of land north of the Savannah River in Augusta, Georgia, and excited at the prospect of working for this reputable company, Watson hitchhiked to Georgia to apply for a job with absolutely no money. Fortunately, he was offered a position in process control instrumentation, a field with which he was totally unfamiliar. But his knowledge of science and physics might have been of interest to his employer. After accepting the job, DuPont transferred Watson and seven other new employees to Pensacola, Florida, to calibrate instruments in a nylon plant that the chemical company was building for Chemstrand Corporation.

David Watson

Following his employment at Dupont, Watson journeyed to Philadelphia, where he was hired as an instrumentation engineer at Brown Instrument, a division of Minneapolis-based Honeywell Corporation. After having worked with Honeywell for two years, Dryomatic Corporation in Alexander, Virginia, recruited Watson. Here, he became the design engineer and plant manager for two years.

A few years later, Watson and three other employees started a desiccant dehumidifier manufacturing company in Alexandria, which they named Universal Dynamics Corporation, where he became machine designer and plan superintendent. Desiccant dehumidifiers help control the humidity and all issues associated with it by providing a cleaner hygienic environment. Importantly, Universal Dynamics supplied dehumidifiers for the government machine tool layaway program known as the Atlas missile sites and any other application that required a dry atmosphere.

During his nine-year association with the company, ABS plastic was introduced in the marketplace. Watson described ABS plastic as high-impact plastic used for kick plates, vacuum cleaners, and a myriad of other applications.

As Universal Dynamics' only machine designer, owing to its smaller size, Watson's machine design used a new desiccant called micro traps that was successful. Hoppers were placed on the throat of plastic extruders and injection-molding machines, and hot, dehumidified air from his machines circulated up through the plastic, thereby rendering it dry. Because of its success, it created a ready market for Universal Dynamics hopper dryers.

After nine very successful years with Universal Dynamics, Watson became restless and decided there was little romance in selling dry air. This prompted him to sell his stock to his partners prior to being recruited by Greensboro, North Carolina-based Wysong Miles Company, a manufacturer of metal shears and bending rolls. Watson was named eastern regional sales manager, with a territory from South

Carolina to Maine. Because of his success at Wysong Miles, Watson achieved the biggest sales increase in the history of the company since its inception in 1905.

Making Vacuum Cleaners

Following his twenty-two years of success at Wyson Miles, Richmond-based B.T. Crump, a manufacturer of harnesses and hassocks, recruited him. Since Kirby Vacuum Cleaner Company of Cleveland, Ohio, had patented a hassock vacuum cleaner, Watson was hired to take over the final design, production, and sales of the vacuum cleaner. Unfortunately, Crump went bankrupt because of its financial condition. All was not lost, however, as Kirby awarded its patent rights to the vacuum cleaner and gave Watson stock in the company.

Home vacuum cleaners were sold primarily through department stores, a fact that prompted Macy's to buy the product, but the vacuum cleaner failed in the marketplace.

Laser Machine-Prima 5000 watts

Having successfully engaged in machine tool sales at Wysong Miles Company, Watson and a partner opened a machine tool dealership covering the states of North and South Carolina and Virginia, a dealership they owned and operated. During their more than two decades of ownership of their new company, Watson and his partners proved to be very successful in machine tool sales, causing many of their companies to reach number one status.

A New Entrepreneur at Sixty-Five

At sixty-five years of age and following four decades of success as a machine engineer and designer, plant superintendent, and salesman, Watson became an entrepreneur in 1992 after having sold his stock in Wysong Miles to his partners and formed Watson Machine Corporation, which is currently located in eastern Powhatan County, west of Richmond. After its creation, Watson made one of his sons, Sam, president of the new venture. Watson had complete confidence in Sam's ability to operate the new company that engaged in sheet metal fabrication. However, Sam died some thirteen years after having become president of Watson Machine from what Watson said was "sloppy surgery."

After having picked Sam as president of Watson Machine, Watson helped his second son, David, begin Southland Machine Tool Company, a machine tool distributorship. Both companies continue to excel in their respective fields. David has ranked number one for ten different suppliers.

In one sense, the creation of Watson Machine in 1992 represented the culmination of David Watson's outstanding forty-some year career in the fabrication and machine tool industry. Today, Watson's company enjoys an excellent reputation among its customers. Calling Watson Machine Company a laser shop, Watson said its fabrication or metal cutting is done by laser beams that hold very close tolerances and cut within two-thousandths of an inch over the entire bed of the machine. The current president of Watson Machine, Justin Antrobius, said, "We fabricate raw metal into a finished product, using the latest cutting, bending, rolling, and welding machines."

Watson said, "Being a custom metal fabricator encompasses manufacturing thousands of different parts with thicknesses, from shim stock to three-quarters inch plate." But his customers appreciate the fact that they produce parts to their tolerances not requiring rejection and remanufacturing of the parts.

Laser Machine-Bystonic 4400 watts

Employee Recognition

David Watson loves his business and frequently praises his loyal employees, a few of whom are Vietnamese. Jokingly, he said his late son, Sam, referred to the five Vietnamese men who worked for him as his "foreign legion." He and his wife, Marie, are deeply religious people and practice their Christian faith and the Golden Rule every day of their lives.

During an interview with Watson, I learned the employees are paid monthly bonuses based on the profit of the previous month. In addition and, very importantly, they also share the proceeds from the sale of scrap metal with their employees. Due largely to its excellent employee relations, Watson's company rarely experiences any employee turnover. During our interview concerning plant operations and the history of his company, he frequently praised his employees and, very importantly, his customers.

Stressing the importance with which he places on his employees, Mr. Watson provided an article written by Jeffrey Gitomer, president of a Charlotte, North Carolina, company that conducts training programs on sales and customer service. It said:

> I find it amazing that companies spend thousands of training dollars on policy, rules, and customer service—but if the boss is a jerk and the internal atmosphere is lousy, the training is worthless, and the company goes nowhere. And the boss blames everyone else except himself.[43]

Watson Machine Company takes additional steps to evaluate and retain good employees. For example, in order to place a new prospective employee in a position that is commensurate with his or her talents, the company uses a personality analysis to determine basic aptitude. The test is underpinned by the idea that human beings enjoy work when it is commensurate with the talents of the new employee. Therefore, Watson added, "Don't put a square peg in a round hole." He also used a colorful analogy, "Ducks are gracious swimming in the water whereas chickens in the water become frustrated."

During the period in which he manufactured desiccant dryers, Watson learned that James Lincoln, president of Lincoln Electric, evaluated his employees on the concept of incentive management. At the end of each year, each person was paid a bonus based on the employee's cooperation, productivity, and absentee record. Amazingly, some people actually made more in bonuses than they did in salary. Even a half-century after starting its incentive management concept, Lincoln is a worldwide company using the same principles with their people. Importantly, Watson's company continues to pattern its employee relationship on the Lincoln incentive management program.

Indicating his disappointment at some business owners, Watson cannot understand the reason why people risk investment capital to start a business, rent a building, hire employees, set up books, purchase equipment, install telephones, advertise to make the telephone ring, and then refuse to answer the phone or, upon answering, screen the call or act rude to the caller.

Watson believes the result of this type of behavior is that dissatisfied employees and customers are a sure formula for failure.

A Very Successful Metal Fabricator

During its history, Watson Machine has gained an enviable reputation among businesses that require manufacturing skills but also possesses depth of management and specialized talents that this very successful metal fabrication company has demonstrated over its two decades in its industry that are due largely to the career path of David Watson.

According to Hoover.com, an online service that profiles various industries, "The United States fabricated metal parts industry includes about fifty-five thousand companies with about $340 billion in combined annual revenue." As is the case in many other industries, the fabrication business is fragmented with the largest companies, a few of whom are Ball Corporation, Flowserve, Mueller Industries, Snap-On, and Timken, comprising about 20 percent of revenue.[44]

Mansel Blackford's excellent book on the history of small business in America featured a subchapter entitled "Successful Small Metal Manufacturers," which referred to characteristics that could have been intended to describe the culture at Watson Machine. While this particular chapter discusses small metal companies in the late nineteenth century, Blackford wrote:

> Consciously or unconsciously, the small manufacturers adopted a growth strategy that would

remain one of the keys to success in small business into the late twentieth century: they developed specialty products which they then sold in niche markets, thereby often avoiding direct competition with their larger counterparts.[45]

Moreover, Blackford wrote, in words that could describe Watson Machine, "Running the companies were managers (who were) deeply committed to their success. Most of the companies, even those organized as corporations, continued to be operated as family enterprises."

Very importantly, Blackford wrote:

More than a quest for profits animated their owners. A sense of personal satisfaction, almost a sense of craftsmanship, remained an important motivating factor for their executives and workers ... Not surprisingly, personal connections and informal ways of conducting business continued to be important in the daily operation of the firms ... Many of the entrepreneurs of these niche companies were managers who were deeply committed to their success (with most of them) operated as family enterprises.[46]

Companies such as Watson Machine provide good reason to believe that American industry can continue to generate superior products that will boost overall economic productivity. America's ability to boost growth and employment depends on it. In fact, Mark Perry, economics professor at the University of Michigan and a visiting scholar at the American Enterprise Institute, wrote in an article in the February 26, 2011 *Wall Street Journal* in which he said that the empirical evidence indicates that America has:

> [A] thriving and growing US manufacturing sector, and a country that remains by far the world's larger manufacturer ... The average US factory worker is responsible for more than $180,000 of annual manufacturing output, triple the $60,000 in 1972 ... These increases are a direct result of capital investments in productivity-enhancing technology.[47]

The latter of which is the kind that the able employees at Watson Machine makes and utilizes for its valued customers.

Al Katz, Retirement Community and Nursing Home President

The labor of my love.

Living above the family grocery store in Durham, North Carolina, with his four sisters and two brothers following the death of his father, Morris, when he was two years of age, taught Al Katz some valuable lessons in life. First, he grew to appreciate the wisdom of the advice of his mother, Lena, and her untiring love for her children. In fact, Katz smiled as he quoted some of the words from his mother that he has never forgotten. "There is so much good in the worst of us and so much bad in the best of us that it hardly behooves any of us to talk about the rest of us."

Second, his father's death allowed his oldest brother, Gilbert, to become an important role model in his life. In fact, his brother was admitted to Duke University on a scholarship because of his wrestling ability. Katz always looked up to Gilbert, who joined the air force as a pilot in December 1941, a few days after Pearl Harbor. Katz himself joined the Navy in 1944.

In addition to his brother's positive influence, his father's death made Katz aware of the need to obtain a college education to provide the knowledge for job skills that he would require later in life. Fully aware of his mother's efforts to support her family from the income from the grocery store, Katz grew to appreciate her enormous sacrifices for the family and the need to help others in life. His synagogue and rabbi in Richmond became a source of spiritual enrichment to him in life.

Following his graduation from the University of North Carolina with a bachelor of science degree in finance, Katz moved to Richmond, where he met his future wife, Doris. Both continued their education at the University of Richmond's evening college where Katz completed additional courses in accounting and finance, both of which prepared him for the position of CFO at Meridian Electronics and Harvey's Warehouse in Richmond. He resigned from Harvey's in 1981.

Raising Funds for Nursing Home

Working in finance in a retail environment did not present the kind of real challenge that Katz desired in life. Coincidentally, in the late 1970s, an executive friend from Richmond-based Reynolds Metals Corporation asked him to join the budget and finance committee for Beth Sholom, the only Jewish nursing home in Richmond. He would later become its CEO.

A group of local Jewish philanthropic leaders in 1945 created Beth Sholom on the Boulevard in Richmond's historic Fan district as World War II was nearing an end. The original Beth Sholom home provided quality care for thirty-four residents, and it was the first Jewish home for the elderly in Virginia. In fact, elderly Jewish patients from the Tidewater area of Virginia shared the Richmond facility for a brief period until they were fortunate to have their own nursing home and apartment complex in the 1980s.

Al Katz

A decade later in 1955 and with a growing waiting list, Beth Sholom moved to Henrico County at Libbie and Fitzhugh Avenues, where it constructed a facility that consisted of fifty beds that, in the next decade, expanded to one hundred and sixteen rooms in 1965. By the 1970s, combined with passage of Medicare and Medicaid, a new master plan was prepared to meet the increased needs of the Jewish elderly.

Given Katz's knowledge and experience in finance, he was the ideal candidate to engage in fund-raising that would provide quality health care for Richmond's elderly Jewish population. Furthermore, after he became president of Beth Sholom on a voluntary basis in 1978, Katz and the CEO, Ira Robbins, developed a financial plan to pay for the purchase of additional land in Henrico County's far west end for future growth. Beth Sholom's board of directors later approved the purchase of the west end property.

Following the approval by the board, Katz and Larry Gelford, who was CEO of Beth Sholom from 1983 to 1988, launched fund raising activities that generated in excess of $2 million dollars and simultaneously led efforts to sell the old nursing home at Libbie and Fitzhugh Ave. in Richmond.

Beth Sholom Gardens

Buying Computers from Ross Perot

After Katz became CFO in 1981, he was keenly aware that Beth Sholom needed an expansion and upgrade of its information processing or computer facilities. Accordingly, he supervised the installation of a new innovative computer system from Electronic Data Systems (EDS) for Beth Sholom that he purchased on a trip to Dallas from Ross Perot, the billionaire founder of the Texas-based company who later became a candidate for president in 1992 against George H.W. Bush.

Following his seven-year position as CFO, Katz was appointed CEO in 1988, a position he held for ten years, that elevated him to head of the entire health care facilities, strategic planning and capital, and operating budgets at all of the facilities.

Some leaders personify a different type of entrepreneur or risk taker despite the fact they did not start a business venture at its birth. In fact, many of these talented individuals have the ability to elevate a business to a higher stage of growth. Katz labeled his career with Beth Sholom as "the labor of my love," and his significant fund-raising efforts took the entire health care and living facility, which had long been located in the near west end, to a new and important level.

As CEO of Beth Sholom in 1988, Katz supervised three hundred and fifty employees and administrators at its facilities, which included special units for memory-impaired patients and skilled care units for residents requiring transition from a hospital setting and home health care. Importantly, since his mother-in-law was a resident at Beth Sholom, his leadership role had special meaning.

Housed on approximately sixteen acres, the wooded Beth Sholom Lifecare Community consists of a one hundred and sixteen-bed nursing home, a sixty-unit assisted living residence known as the Gardens, which opened on November 1, 2000, a one-hundred-and-eleven-apartment complex known as the Woods, and an outpatient rehabilitation Clinic that offers outpatient physical, occupational, and speech therapies. In addition, a second assisted living facility named Parkside was completed in the summer of 2011 under the current leadership of CEO Mark Finkle.

Importantly, activities and services are provided on- and off-site in some areas to residents. Other services include a dementia and Alzheimer's unit, on-site nursing and physician services, occupational therapy services, podiatry services, and many other activities and services for residents.

Getting the Best Employees

During his leadership of the retirement and health care facility, Katz fully understood and practiced the importance of satisfying the customer or, as in his case, the patients or residents of his nursing homes. For example, during the interview process for new employees, he instructed persons working in the human resource department to ask new applicants if they liked themselves. Surprisingly, he discovered some of them had a very low self-esteem, which Katz viewed as an indication of an individual who would not be the best caregiver for nursing home residents. He was especially keen on providing the best care possible for the residents since their happiness and satisfaction affected the future of Beth Sholom.

Entrance to Facilities.

In addition to his executive positions with Beth Sholom, Katz has served as:

- A member of the board of directors of Bon Secours of Richmond

- A member of the board of Bon Secours Assisted Living Facility

- A member of Service Corps of Retired Executives (SCORE), a nonprofit association that provides counseling for individuals who desire to start a business

- A member of the board of Beth Sholom Garden's Assisted Living Facility

During his nearly twenty years working at Beth Sholom, Al Katz demonstrated the fund-raising and managerial talents to take this top-quality facility to new levels. Given the increasing need for quality health care, facilities like Beth Sholom will be more important in the future.

According to a 2008 report from the Bureau of Labor Statistics, nursing home and residential care facilities for the elderly provide nearly 18 percent of all employment in the health care industry.[48] In the next decade, employment in this sector of the industry is estimated to increase to 21.2 percent. The latest information on the number of nursing homes in the United States, according to Medicare.gov, indicates approximately seventeen thousand of these facilities are in the United States.[49]

Even with the passage of ObamaCare, it is doubtful that spending on health care will decline. In fact, owing to the aging of the US population, the need for facilities such as Beth Sholom and leaders with the skills of an Al Katz will increase in the future.

Epilogue

I could not have written this book without the cooperation of the sixteen entrepreneurs in this book, those risk takers who embraced change and invested their capital, time, and effort to build successful enterprises that have improved the lives of not only themselves but their customers and employees as well. My book is a celebration of their long journeys, many of which were not easy ones, particularly during the Great Recession of 2008–2010. Importantly, I hope our political leaders will be supportive of entrepreneurs and refrain from placing any unnecessary impediments in their paths.

I am also grateful to my wife, who encouraged me to write about entrepreneurs. Her patience and support helped to sustain me through the many weeks and months that it took to complete this project. I also want to thank my son, Tom, who suggested I write about a few of the entrepreneurs in this book as well as his wife, Ceci, who helped me with the inclusion of photographs in the chapters. Lastly, I want to thank the talented editors at iUniverse who helped me produce a much, much better book than the original manuscript that I submitted in the spring of 2011.

Starting a new business is not an easy endeavor. As I stated in the Introduction and as indicated in Carol Roth's new best-seller on entrepreneurs that I also cited, most new small businesses do not survive. Roth wrote, "It's all about executing a viable business model (and realizing that) the secret to a successful business is hard, focused work."

Amid their successes, it is doubtful that the entrepreneurs featured in this book could have done it alone. In addition to the hard work necessary to become successful, some of the entrepreneurs featured in this book benefited from being at the right place at the right time, the critical importance of family and friends, the benefit of living in a culture that is favorable to free market capitalism and the talents and labor of their employees. Indeed, these factors compliment the enormous personal skills of the entrepreneurs whose efforts were responsible for the success of their own enterprises.

Given the difficulties that confront entrepreneurs, we must admire the courage and risks they confront on a daily basis and applaud those who have survived recessions, the changing trends, and fierce competition in markets, overcoming the difficulty of hiring enough competent and loyal employees and being able to be right about the future most of the time.

In an important article published by the *Wall Street Journal* on April 12, 2011, Vinton Cerf, who helped develop the Internet as a pioneer in data networking technology and is Google's chief Internet evangelist, wrote, "Despite our well-developed college and post-college system, America simply is not producing enough of our innovators." He attributed this to a K–12 educational system that needs improvement and "a national culture that does not emphasize the value of engineering and science."

Moreover, he added, "The American public focuses more on sports and entertainment figures and less on the scientists and engineers whose innovations make our lives easier, safer, healthier, and more productive."[50]

Very importantly, I want this book to inspire and encourage would-be entrepreneurs, including students in high schools and colleges, to embark on journeys similar to the risk takers in this book and to be part of Adam Smith's famous invisible hand as much as possible. The courage to continue after mistakes or failure, embrace change and innovation, engage in long-range planning, adopt a realistic business plan, and not fear hard work, these are some of the factors required to be a successful entrepreneur. Go for it. You will be joining many successful businesspeople who have improved the financial well-being of their lives, provided jobs for their employees, boosted economic growth in their localities, states, and even the entire nation, created great products or services, and improved their communities in many important ways.

Bibliography

Akerloff, Robert, and Robert J. Skiller. *Animal Spirits: How Modern Psychology Drives the Economy and Why it Matters for Global Capitalism*. Princeton: Princeton University Press, 2009.

Blackford, Mansel G. *A History of Small Business in America*. Chapel Hill and London: The University of North Carolina Press, 2003.

Croslin, David. *Innovate the Future: A Radical Approach to IT Innovation*. Upper Saddle River, N.J., Prentice Hall, 2010.

Laffer, Arthur, and Stephen Moore. *Return to Prosperity: How America Can Regain Its Economic Superpower Status*. New York: Threshold Editions, 2010.

Levengood, Paul. *Virginia: Catalyst of Commerce for Four Centuries*. Encino, Calif.: Cherbo Publishing Group, Inc., 2006.

Luecke, Richard. *Entrepreneur's Tool Kit: Tips and Techniques to Grow Your Business*. Boston: Harvard Business School Publishing Corp., 2005.

Masterson, Michael. *Ready, Fire, and Aim*. Hoboken, N.Y.: John Wiley & Sons, 2008.

Peters, Tom. *Circle of Innovation*. New York: Signet Books, 1997.

Rand, Ayn. *Atlas Shrugged*. New York: Signet Books, 1957.

Roth, Carol. *Entrepreneur Equation*. Dallas: BenBellaBooks, 2011.

Schumpeter, Joseph. *Capitalism, Socialism, and Democracy*. New York: Harper, 1975.

Smith, Adam. *Money Game*. New York: Random House, 1968.

Smith, Adam. *The Wealth of Nations*. New York: A Bantam Book, 2003.

Note: The above-referenced *Money Game* was actually written by George J.W. Goodman, but wrote the book under the pseudonym of "Adam Smith." See chapter 2 on David Ward.

Notes

1. Adam Smith, *The Wealth of Nations* (New York: Bantam Book, 2003), xvii.
2. Art Laffer and Stephen Moore, *Return to Prosperity: How America Can Regain Its Superpower Status* (New York: Threshold Editions, 2010), 148.
3. Laffer and Moore, 148.
4. Joseph Schumpeter, *Capitalism, Socialism and Democracy* (New York: Harper, 1975), 88.
5. Tom Peters, *Circle of Innovation* (New York: Alfred Knopf, 1997), xvi.
6. Mansel Blackford, *A History of Small Business in America* (Chapel Hill and London: The University of North Carolina Press, 2003), 3.
7. Blackford, 3.
8. Carol Hazard, "Snag-a-Job Wins Praise from SBA during Henrico Visit," *Richmond Times-Dispatch*, March 2011, 18.
9. Blackford, 181.
10. Blackford, 181.
11. Blackford, 179.
12. Peters, 104.
13. *Entrepreneur*, "Be Disruptive," January 2011, 20.
14. "David Croslin: Business of Reinvention," www.phoenix.edu/alumni/phoenix-focus/2011/03/david-croslin-business-of-reinvention.html
15. "David Croslin: Business of Reinvention"
16. "Restoring the American Dream," March 6, 2011 (CNN special with Fareed Zakaria).
17. Ayn Rand, *Atlas Shrugged* (New York: Signet, 1957), 978.
18. Carol Roth, *Entrepreneur Equation* (Dallas: BenbellaBooks, 2011), 2.
19. Roth, 19.
20. www.roll-call.com/about-irc/history-of-irc.aspx.
21. "Donald Trump: How to Hear 'You're Hired,'" http://jobs.aol.com/articles/2011/01/27/donald-trump-career-advice

22. http://urbanviewsweekly.com/2011/01/19/today%2%/80%/99%-power-broker

23. http://manta.com/mb 45 AA15D000 47/building maintenance services nec/ Virginia

24. www.ibisworld.com/industry/default.aspx?indid=1496

25. www.hoovers.com/industry/janitorial-services-carpet-cleaning/1905-1.html

26. "David Croslin: Business of Reinvention"

27. "Google Search NAA Auction," www.sellwithauctions-briefhistory

28. http://econport.org/econport/request?page=man auctions-briefhistory

29. http://auctiontecs.com/auctionsphp

30. Mark Motley, "Master of going, going, gone: the real story," *Richmond Times-Dispatch*, April 30, 2007.

31. Laffer and Moore, 148.

32. Laffer and Moore, 148.

33. "Be Disruptive," *Entrepreneur*, January 2011, 20.

34. http://wikipedia.org/wiki/HVAC

35. www.ibisworld.com/industry/default.aspx?indid=1945

36. www.fluidsolutionsinc.com/HVAC.htm

37. www.hoovers.com/industry/electrical-contractors/1857-1.html

38. Blackford, 87.

39. www.American Staffing.net/statistics/historical-data.cfm

40. www.firstresearch.com/Industry-Research/Catering-Services.html

41. www.firstresearch.com/Industry-Research/Catering-Services.html

42. Laffer and Moore, 148.

43. Jeffrey Gitmer, "Which Comes First, the Chicken or the Boss?" *IB the Experts*, 2001.

44. www.hoovers.com/industry/metal-fabrication/1401-1.hmtl

45. Blackford, 88.

46. Blackford, 88.

47. Mark Perry, "The Truth About Manufacturing," *The Wall Street Journal*, February 26, 2011, 15.

48. www.bls.gov/oco/cq/cqs035.htm

49. http://medicare.gov/nursing/overview.asp

50. Vincent Cerf, "Firing Up American Innovation," *The Wall Street Journal*, April 12, 2011, 15.

Open Book Editions
A Berrett-Koehler Partner

Open Book Editions is a joint venture between Berrett-Koehler Publishers and Author Solutions, the market leader in self-publishing. There are many more aspiring authors who share Berrett-Koehler's mission than we can sustainably publish. To serve these authors, Open Book Editions offers a comprehensive self-publishing opportunity.

A Shared Mission

Open Book Editions welcomes authors who share the Berrett-Koehler mission—Creating a World That Works for All. We believe that to truly create a better world, action is needed at all levels—individual, organizational, and societal. At the individual level, our publications help people align their lives with their values and with their aspirations for a better world. At the organizational level, we promote progressive leadership and management practices, socially responsible approaches to business, and humane and effective organizations. At the societal level, we publish content that advances social and economic justice, shared prosperity, sustainability, and new solutions to national and global issues.

Open Book Editions represents a new way to further the BK mission and expand our community. . We look forward to helping more authors challenge conventional thinking, introduce new ideas, and foster positive change.

For more information, see the Open Book Editions website: http://www.iuniverse.com/Packages/OpenBookEditions.aspx

Join the BK Community! See exclusive author videos, join discussion groups, find out about upcoming events, read author blogs, and much more! http://bkcommunity.com/